Whispers of the Wild

Whispers of the Wild

Joel Hawksley

J&Washington

CONTENTS

Dedicated to anyone who has the heart of a lion, the wisdom of an owl, and the grace of a gazelle.

To those with the cunning of a fox, the strength of a tiger, and the resilience of a polar bear. For the brave souls who navigate life like a wolf, possess the patience of a tortoise, and the determination of a beaver.

May you embody the elegance of a swan, the endurance of an elephant, and the playfulness of a sea otter. May you soar with the freedom of an eagle, embrace the gentleness of a deer, and exude the charm of a hummingbird.

To the dreamers with the curiosity of a raccoon, the agility of a leopard, and the spirit of a dolphin. You who reflect the loyalty of a dog, the wisdom of a turtle, and the wonder of a butterfly.

This book is for you, the extraordinary blend of the wild's finest traits, whose journey inspires us all."

Introduction

In this heartwarming collection of poems, I, aim to whisk you away on a lyrical safari through a vibrant canopy of life on Earth. From the red panda's playful swagger to the koi's quiet grace, each creature is brought to life with vivid descriptions and delightful rhymes.

But these poems are more than just playful portraits. I intend to ignite a spark of wonder and connection with the animal kingdom within you. As you delve into these pages, I hope you'll discover:

- **The enduring strength of resilience:** Be inspired by the tenacious spirit of the salamander, who can regenerate and adapt even after fire.

- **The boundless joy of curiosity:** Embrace the world with the wide-eyed wonder of the inquisitive raccoon, forever exploring and uncovering nature's secrets.

- **The importance of community:** Find comfort and strength in the togetherness of the capybara families or the playful bonds between dolphins.

Whether you're a seasoned animal enthusiast or simply someone who appreciates the beauty of the natural world, these poems offer a unique perspective on the creatures we share our planet with. They are a delightful introduction to the power of poetry and a gentle reminder of the valuable lessons we can learn from the animal kingdom.

1

The Majestic Cats

Lion, Tiger, Leopard, Cheetah,

Lynx, Florida Panther

Lion

With mane of gold and muscles bold,
The lion stands, a king of old.
His roar a challenge, loud and clear,
Inspiring courage, casting out fear.

**Let courage be our guiding light,
To face the shadows, fight for what's right.
Don't shrink from battles, big or small,
Like lions, rise and conquer all.**

The lioness, a huntress keen,
Provides and protects, a regal queen.
With cunning tactics, patience deep,
She stalks her prey, her secrets keeps.

**Let strategy be wisdom's tool,
To plan with foresight, act when cool.
Like lionesses, strong and bright,
We'll hunt for knowledge, claim our light.**

In pride they gather, fierce and strong,
A bond of loyalty where they belong.
For family they fight, with all their might,
United hearts that face the night.

**Let loyalty be love's embrace,
To cherish kin, find solace's space.
Like lions, fierce in their defense,
We'll guard our loved ones, with no pretense.**

*So take a page from the lion's plight,
Be brave, be wise, and hold on tight.
With courage, cunning, hearts ablaze,
We'll write our story, in brighter days.*

Tiger

With stripes of fire and silent tread,
The tiger stalks, a king unsaid.
Through sun-dappled leaves, a flash of might,
A hunter's grace in darkest night.

Let stealth be sharp, a hidden art,
To plan with cunning, win our part.
Like tigers, unseen, yet ever near,
We'll strike with purpose, quell our fear.

Unleashed power in muscles coiled,
A fearsome pounce, a story foiled.

Raw strength they wield, a force untold,
Defenders fierce, in nature's fold.

Let courage roar, a steady flame,
To face our fears, and rise to fame.
Like tigers, bold and unafraid,
We'll conquer challenges, dreams are made.

Solitary souls, they claim their ground,
A silent pride, their freedom found.
They stalk alone, yet kin they hold,
A fierce embrace, when danger's cold.

Let independence be our guide,
To forge our path, with hearts inside.
Like tigers, strong and self-assured,
We'll find our way, forever pure.

So take a page from the tiger's might,
Be stealthy, brave, and claim your light.
With cunning plans and fearless heart,
You'll carve your path, and play your part.

Leopard

With patterned coat, a silent blur,
The leopard stalks, unseen, a purr.
Muscles coiled, with power held tight,
It strikes with speed, in fading light.

Let stealth and grace be how we move,
With calculated steps, to win our groove.
Like leopards, silent, swift, and keen,
We'll reach our goals, unseen, pristine.

A solitary hunter bold,
It claims its prize, a story told.

Independence, a spirit strong,
It carves its path, where it belongs.

Let self-reliance be our guide,
To trust ourselves, with nothing to hide.
Like leopards, forging their own way,
We'll stand on our own, come what may.

High in the trees, its trophies rest,
Secured with strength, it puts them to the test.
Resourceful mind, a cunning plan,
It uses all, to make a stand.

Let resourcefulness be our key,
To find solutions, wild and free.
Like leopards, with a clever mind,
We'll waste no chance, what we can find.

So take a hint from the spotted hide,
Be silent, strong, with nothing to hide.
With stealthy steps and cunning soul,
We'll reach our goals, and make life whole.

Cheetah

A blur of spots, a cheetah streaks,
The fastest runner, so it speaks.
With streamlined form and focused gaze,
It chases prey in fleeting daze.

Let focus be our guiding star,
To channel energy, no matter how far.
Like cheetahs, swift and sharp and keen,
We'll chase our goals, a vibrant scene.

Its powerful strides, a blur of grace,
Eat up the ground, a lightning pace.

With bursts of speed and laser sight,
It claims its prize, in pure, white light.

Let decisive action be our call,
To seize the moment, give our all.
Like cheetahs, striking fast and true,
We'll make our choices, see them through.

Though sprinting short, it rests between,
For focused bursts, a vibrant scene.
With pacing planned and purpose clear,
It finds its rhythm, conquers fear.

Let strategic rest our spirits mend,
To rise renewed, until the end.
Like cheetahs, sprinting, then at ease,
We'll find our balance, feel the breeze.

So take a lesson from the cheetah's might,
Be focused, fast, and take to flight.
With channeled energy and bursts of glee,
We'll chase our dreams, and wild and free.

Lynx

With tufted ears and silent stride,
The lynx, unseen, with nature confide.
Sharp eyes they hold, that pierce the night,
A master hunter, swift and light.

**Let focus be our guiding star,
To see with clarity, no matter how far.
Like lynx, with gaze that cuts through haze,
We'll find our path, through life's many maze.**

Huge, padded paws, on silent tread,
They stalk their prey, with watchful head.
Patience they hold, a virtue rare,
To wait for the right time, with cunning snare.

Let patience be our steady hand,
To wait for wisdom, understand.
Like lynx, we'll learn to bide our time,
Until the moment, makes its chime.

Though solitary hunters true,
They share their bond, a loyal crew.
For mates they care, with gentle touch,
A fierceness burns, for loved ones such.

Let fierce protectiveness embrace our soul,
To shield the ones who make us whole.
Like lynx, we'll guard with watchful eye,
The ones we cherish, beneath the sky.

So take a page from the lynx's might,
Be focused, patient, hold on tight.
With watchful eyes and hearts ablaze,
We'll find our purpose, through life's many maze.

Florida Panther

With stealthy paws and coat of night,
The Florida panther, a silent might.
A ghost of beauty, rare and sleek,
Through shadowed swamps, its secrets leak.

Let mystery be your guiding light,
Unveil the depths, with all your might.
Like panthers, silent, unseen, unheard,
Discover truths, by whispered word.

They stalk their prey with senses keen,
A hunter's grace, a jungle queen.

With lightning strikes and lightning leaps,
They claim their prize, where darkness sleeps.

Let focus be your inner flame,
To chase your dreams, and fan life's game.
Like panthers, eyes that pierce the night,
Set goals ablaze, with focused might.

Though solitary paths they roam,
A watchful eye protects their home.
With fierce defense, their young they tend,
A mother's love, that knows no end.

Let protectiveness be your embrace,
To shield what's dear, in every space.
Like panthers, guarding all they hold,
Keep what you cherish, brave and bold.

But dangers lurk, their numbers fall,
A fading echo, nature's call.
Let's mend the harm, and set them free,
The Florida panther, wild and key.

So take a stand, with hearts alight,
Protect their shadows, hold on tight.
With watchful eyes and purpose true,
The Florida panther's future, we'll renew.

2

The Wild Dogs

*Wolf, Coyote, Fox, Dingo,
Golden Jackal, African Wild Dog*

Wolf

In frosted fur, a leader bold,
The wolf survives, a story told.
With packmates close, a loyal band,
They hunt and thrive, across the land.

Let strength in unity be our guide,
In teams we prosper, side by side.
Like wolves, together fierce and strong,
We'll face all trials, where we belong.

Their piercing howls, a chorus deep,
Communicate across the sleep.
With clear intent and voices true,
Their message rings, for all to view.

Let honest speech be ever clear,
With open hearts, cast out all fear.
Like wolves, their message, loud and strong,
We'll speak our truth, to right all wrong.

They train their young with patient care,
To hunt and live, a burden to share.
With knowledge passed, from old to new,
The pack endures, forever true.

Let mentorship be wisdom's share,
To guide the young, with love and care.
Like wolves, who teach with watchful eye,
We'll share our knowledge, reaching high.

So take a page from the wolf's proud line,
Be strong, be loyal, let your purpose shine.
With pack mentality, hearts ablaze,
We'll build a future, through all our days.

Coyote

The coyote trots, a cunning soul,
With amber eyes and fur of gold.
A trickster spirit, wild and free,
Adapts and thrives, for all to see.

Let resourcefulness be our guide,
To find new paths, where none reside.
Like coyotes, clever and keen,
We'll find solutions, unseen, unforeseen.

They stalk their prey with silent stride,
Using the shadows, on their cunning side.
Patience and planning, their tactics unfold,
A lesson in strategy, worth more than gold.

Let strategy be our inner map,
To think ahead, and avoid mishap.
Like coyotes, cunning and wise,
We'll plan our course, beneath thoughtful skies.

Though seeming solitary at times they roam,
Family ties call them back to home.
With playful pups and loyal mates,
They share their bounty, through life's cruel fates.

Let loyalty be our guiding star,
For those we cherish, no matter how far.
Like coyotes, fierce and true,
We'll stand by loved ones, see them through.

Their howls ring out, a haunting cry,
Communicating, beneath the vast, night sky.
A chorus strong, a message bold,
Unity and kinship, stories untold.

Let communication be our bridge to build,
With open hearts and thoughts revealed.
Like coyotes, voices reaching far,
We'll share our truths, beneath a guiding star.

So take a cue from the coyote's might,
Be clever, plan, and fight for what's right.
With cunning spirit and hearts ablaze,
We'll navigate life's twists and desert's maze.

Fox

With eyes of amber, sharp and sly,
the fox is cunning, with a knowing eye.
It hunts by wit, not brute force pure,
A master strategist, forever sure.

Let cunning be our mental might,
To solve life's puzzles, set things right.
Like foxes, plans well thought and keen,
We'll outsmart troubles, on life's sharp scene.

A solitary soul, it walks alone,
Yet fiercely loyal to those it's known.

For family, love burns bright and deep,
A hidden fire, secrets they keep.

Let loyalty with trust entwine,
In chosen bonds, a love that's thine.
Like foxes, fierce in their defense,
We'll guard our loved ones, with no pretense.

By night they stalk, unseen, unheard,
A silent hunter, with every word.
Adaptability, their truest art,
They blend and change, to play their part.

Let flexibility be our guide,
To bend with life, with open stride.
Like foxes, changing with the flow,
We'll find new paths, where good things grow.

So take a wisdom from the fox's den,
Be sharp, be loyal, like trusted kin.
With cunning hearts and minds ablaze,
We'll navigate life's winding maze.

Dingo

With coat of gold and amber bright,
The dingo strides, beneath the southern light.
A song of ages, in their mournful cry,
An ancient spirit, beneath the endless sky.

Let heritage be your guiding light,
Embrace your past, with all your might.
Like dingoes, bound to lands untold,
Carry your history, brave and bold.

They stalk their prey, with senses keen,
Hunters and wanderers, on the outback scene.
A vital link, in nature's chain,
But conflict arises, with brought-in strain.

Let balance be your guiding hand,
To find your place, across the land.
Like dingoes, seeking harmony's call,
Respect the wild, for one and all.

Though howls may echo, misunderstood,
A loyalty fierce, within their blood.
Family bonds, that tightly hold,
Protecting pups, with stories old.

Let kinship be your guiding light,
To cherish those, in day and night.
Like dingoes, fierce for kin they know,
Stand by your loved ones, watch them grow.

But challenges mount, their future unclear,
Fencing divides, and dangers near.
Let's find a way, for them to roam,
And safeguard wild hearts, forever home.

So take a cue from the dingo's might,
Be strong and ancient, hold on tight.
With spirit wild and hearts set free,
Leave paw prints deep, eternally.

Golden Jackal

The golden jackal, lean and keen,
A desert's whisper, rarely seen.
He scents the air, with nose so fine,
Discovering chances, truly divine.

Let opportunism be our keenest sense,
To seize the moment, with no pretense.
Like golden jackals, quick to see,
We'll find our openings, wild and free.

Through rocky trails and sandy dunes,
He finds his sustenance 'neath suns and moons.
No wasted effort, no chance ignored,
From what is given, his life's restored.

Let resourcefulness be our guiding hand,
To make the most of what's at command.
Like golden jackals, making do,
We'll thrive and prosper, seeing us through.

A haunting cry, a distant call,
Connecting voices, standing tall.
For kin he works, with purpose clear,
Dispelling silence, banishing fear.

Let connection be our strong embrace,
To reach out widely, across time and space.
Like golden jackals, voices heard,
We'll build our bonds, on every word.

So take a lesson from the jackal's way,
Be sharp and clever, come what may.
With keen perception, and bonds so true,
You'll navigate life, and see it through.

African Wild Dog

The African Wild Dog, a vibrant coat,
A painted hunter, by teamwork afloat.
In synchronized chase, they flow as one,
A family strong, beneath the sun.

**Let cooperation be our guiding light,
To work as one, with all our might.**

Like wild dogs, harmonious and keen,
We'll achieve our goals, on life's grand scene.

With boundless energy, they roam and play,
A joyful spirit, lighting up their day.
No moment wasted, no effort spared,
For every member, love is shared.

Let enthusiasm drive our stride,
With zest for life, with nothing to hide.
Like wild dogs, vibrant and so free,
We'll find our joy, for all to see.

They share their bounty, feed the weak,
A communal bond, lessons they speak.
No one is left, no one behind,
A loyal spirit, deeply entwined.

Let compassion be our gentle hand,
To lift up others, across the land.
Like wild dogs, nurturing and kind,
We'll leave no one broken, no one behind.

So take a lesson from the wild dog's heart,
Work as a team, play your vital part.
With joyful spirit and empathy's grace,
You'll build a better world, in every place.

3 | Bears and Their Relatives

Bear, Polar Bear, Red Panda, Giant Panda

Bear

In forests deep, where shadows lie,
The mighty bear, with watchful eye.
A lumbering form, with fur so thick,
A gentle giant, or a hunter quick.

Let strength be yours, with wisdom too,
A powerful force, with heart both true.
Like bears, that stand on land and roam,
Find inner power, to bring you home.

They search for berries, sweet and bright,
Or fish in streams, with focused might.
With keenest sense of smell they track,
A feast to find, a hidden snack.

Let focus be your guiding light,
To set your sights, and hold on tight.
Like bears, with purpose clear and strong,
Pursue your goals, where you belong.

Though solitary paths they tread,
For cubs they care, with love well fed.
A watchful mother, fierce and bold,
Protects her young, from stories old.

Let nurturing be your guiding hand,
To cherish those in shifting sand.
Like bears, who teach their cubs to roam,
Guide those you love, and bring them home.

In winter's grip, they slumber deep,
A time for rest, where dreams can creep.
Renewal waits, with spring's first call,
To wake and rise, and stand up tall.

Let resilience be your inner might,
To weather storms, and find the light.
Like bears, emerging strong and new,
Face challenges, and see them through.

So take a page from the bear's strong hand,
Be gentle, fierce, and understand.
With purpose clear and heart alight,
Leave paw prints deep, in day and night.

Polar Bear

With coat of pearl and eyes of black,
The polar bear, a lonely track.
He stalks the ice, a silent king,
Where winter reigns, its harsh winds sing.

**Let resilience be our guiding light,
To face the harshest, hold on tight.
Like polar bears, in endless white,
We'll weather storms, with inner might.**

They hunt for seals with patient grace,
A solitary power, in this frozen space.
With powerful steps and senses keen,
They claim their prize, where life has been.

Let focus be our guiding star,
To set our goals, however far.
Like polar bears, with purpose clear,
We'll chase our dreams, and cast out fear.

Though lonely hunters, some may say,
They raise their cubs in a loving way.
A mother's touch, a fierce embrace,
Protecting young, in this harsh space.

Let nurturing be our gentle hand,
To care and cherish, understand.
Like polar bears, with love that's true,
We'll build a haven, just for you.

But melting ice, a changing scene,
A warming world, a threat unseen.
Their frozen realm, it starts to shrink,
A silent plea, for us to think.

Let awareness be our call to fight,
For balance lost, and fading light.
Like polar bears, a symbol true,
We'll mend the world, for me and you.

So take a page from the bear's lonely plight,
Be strong, be focused, hold on tight.
With hearts that care and voices raised,
We'll build a future, forever praised.

Red Panda

With fur of fire and mask of black,
The red panda, a curious track.
High in the trees, a blushing sight,
A gentle soul, with appetite.

Let passion burn, a vibrant flame,
Embrace your zest, and play life's game.
Like red pandas, with eyes alight,
Pursue your dreams, with all your might.

Their nimble paws on branches cling,
Acrobatic feats, a joyful swing.
With playful spirit, they twist and turn,
A childlike wonder, hearts that yearn.

Let joy be yours, in every climb,
Find playful moments, hold on to time.
Like red pandas, with laughter bright,
Embrace the fun, in morning light.

Though bamboo fills their every bite,
They savor berries, a sweet delight.
Simple pleasures, a mindful art,
Contentment found, within their heart.

Let peacefulness be your guiding light,
Find beauty's essence, day and night.
Like red pandas, in leafy rest,
Find solace deep, within your breast.

(But forests dwindle, a fading dream,
Threats arise, a silent scream.
Let's protect their world, forever green,
The red pandas, a magic scene.)

So take a cue from the red panda's grace,
Be passionate, playful, find your space.
With fiery spirit and heart set free,
Leave paw prints deep, eternally.

Giant Panda

Black and White Playful – (Hēi bái qiào pí)

With coat of black and patches white,
The panda waddles, a curious sight.
Chubby cheeks and eyes so round,
A gentle soul, with bamboo crowned.

Let joy be yours, in black and white,
Find beauty's blend, and hold on tight.
Like pandas, playful, soft, and round,
Embrace all parts, that make you sound.

They munch on bamboo, all day long,
Crunching feast, their happy song.
Simple pleasures, bring content,
A mindful life, truly well spent.

Let peacefulness be your guiding light,
Find joy in moments, ever bright.
Like pandas, chewing, slow and wise,
Savor the present, beneath the skies.

Though solitary paths they roam,
With fellow pandas, they make a home.
Playful tumbles and gentle nuzzles,
A bond of friendship, where love never puzzles.

Let connection be your guiding hand,
To build a love, on shifting sand.
Like pandas, side by side they play,
Find your tribe, and brighten your day.

So take a page from the panda's charm,
Be joyful, peaceful, and free from harm.
With playful spirit and heart so light,
Embrace the world, in black and white.

4

Hoofed Mammals of the Plains

*Zebra, Giraffe, Gazelle, Donkey,
Horse, American Bison,*

Water Buffalo

Zebra

With stripes of black and white so bold,
The zebra grazes, a story told.
In herds they roam, a dazzling sight,
A unity bound by day and night.

Let community be our guiding light,◇
To find our strength, in shared might.
Like zebras, standing side by side,
We'll face the world, in joyful stride.

Their stripes unique, a dazzling blend,
No two the same, from start to end.
Diversity, a vibrant hue,
Strengthens the herd, forever true.

Let acceptance be our open door,
To welcome all, forevermore.
Like zebras, standing close and strong,
We'll celebrate where we belong.

Though skittish sometimes, quick to flee,
They stand their ground, for all to see.
With healthy boundaries, they make a stand,
Respect themselves, across the land.

Let self-respect be our guiding star,
To know our worth, no matter how far.
Like zebras, fierce and ever bold,
We'll claim our space, our story told.

Their black and white, a stark display,
Sees the world in black and white, they say.
With clarity, they choose their fight,
For what is right, with all their might.

Let conviction be our inner flame,
To stand for truth, and speak its name.
Like zebras, stripes of black and white,
We'll fight for justice, with all our might.

So take a lesson from the zebra's herd,
Be strong, united, find your every word.
With open hearts and stripes so bright,
We'll make the world, a dazzling light.

Giraffe

With graceful neck that stretches high,
The giraffe surveys the endless sky.
A gentle giant, calm and wise,
It sees the world with patient eyes.

Let perspective be our guiding light,⟡
To see beyond, with all our might.
Like giraffes, tall and ever keen,
We'll see the big picture, unseen, pristine.

Their long tongues reach for leaves so green,
A constant quest for what's unseen.
With curiosity, ever bold,
They seek out knowledge, stories untold.

Let curiosity be our endless fire,
To ask and learn, with keen desire.
Like giraffes, reaching for the light,
We'll chase new knowledge, day and night.

Though solitary they sometimes roam,
Strong bonds they share, a loving home.
With gentle nudges, soft and slow,
They show affection, in gentle flow.

Let empathy be our compass true,
To feel for others, and see them through.
Like giraffes, reaching out to kind,
We'll build connections, heart and mind.

So take a lesson from the gentle grace,
Be wise, be curious, with gentle embrace.
With open hearts and heads held high,
We'll reach for dreams, beneath the endless sky.

Gazelle

With eyes like jewels and hooves that fly,
The gazelle streaks across the sky.
A dancer's grace on slender frame,
They flee the chase, a whispered name.

Let agility be our guiding light,
To move with swiftness, day and night.
Like gazelles, ever light and quick,
We'll dodge life's hurdles, never stick.

Their leaps defy the earth's embrace,
A soaring spirit, full of grace.
With resilience, they weather the storm,
Enduring hardship, ever warm.

Let adaptability be our key,
To bend and change, as life decrees.
Like gazelles, shifting with the breeze,
We'll find new paths, if trouble appease.

In herds they gather, watchful eyes,
A network strong, where safety lies.
With keen awareness, they sense all near,
A bond of trust, dispelling fear.

Let vigilance be our mindful gaze,
To see the world, through wisdom's haze.
Like gazelles, alert and ever bright,
We'll face the unknown, with all our might.

Though predators may stalk the land,
The gazelle survives, by nature's hand.
With primal instinct, swift and true,
They find their path, a life anew.

Let intuition be our guiding star,
To trust our gut, no matter how far.
Like gazelles, with a dancer's art,
We'll find our rhythm, close to our heart.

So take a lesson from the gazelle's bound,
Be agile, strong, on sacred ground.
With watchful eyes and spirit free,
We'll chase our dreams, eternally.

Donkey

With sturdy frame and patient eyes,
The donkey walks, beneath the skies.
He carries burdens, never complains,
A loyal friend through sun and rains.

Let perseverance be our guiding light,
To bear the weight, and see things right.
Like donkeys, steady, strong, and true,
We'll face our challenges, and see them through.

Though stubborn streaks may sometimes show,
He holds his ground, where others go.

He stands for what he knows is right,
A moral compass, burning bright.

Let integrity be our guiding hand,
To speak our truth, and take a stand.
Like donkeys, firm in their belief,
We'll fight for justice, bring relief.

They graze together, side by side,
A gentle bond, in which they confide.
They share their burdens, never shy,
A friendship built on empathy.

Let compassion be our open door,
To understand, and ask for more.
Like donkeys, feeling others' plight,
We'll ease their burdens, make things right.

So take a page from the donkey's heart,
Be strong, be true, and play your part.
With steady steps and spirit kind,
We'll leave a mark, for all to find.

Horse

With mane of silk and eyes of fire,
The horse, a spirit, full of desire.
A noble creature, strong and proud,
Across the plains, he neighs aloud.

Let freedom be our guiding light,
To run and roam, with all our might.
Like horses, wild and hearts ablaze,
We'll chase our dreams through life's sweet maze.

They stand in power, muscles bold,
A loyal friend, a story told.

With trusting eyes and gentle touch,
They offer freedom, oh so much.

Let partnership be our guiding hand,
To build a bond, on shifting sand.
Like horse and rider, side by side,
We'll face the world, in fearless stride.

They race with wind, a fleeting sight,
A blur of hooves in morning light.
With endless grace and boundless might,
They push their limits, take to flight.

Let determination be our flame,
To chase our goals, and overcome the same.
Like horses, never ones to quit,
We'll reach our targets, bit by bit.

So take a cue from the horse's run,
Be free and strong, beneath the sun.
With hearts that yearn and spirits fleet,
We'll gallop on, with joyful beat.

African Buffalo

With massive horns and iron hide,
The African buffalo strides with pride.
A herd they form, a stoic wall,
Weathered and strong, they face it all.

Let resilience be our guiding star,
To weather storms, no matter how far.
Like buffalo, enduring scars,
We'll rise unbroken, beneath the stars.

Their eyes hold wisdom, deep and old,
Stories etched, in battles bold.
With keen awareness, danger's call,
They stand united, through one and all.

Let vigilance be our watchtower high,
To see the truth, with knowing eye.
Like buffalo, alert and wise,
We'll navigate life's fair disguise.

Though some may see them stubborn and gruff,
They nurture young, with gentle puff.
Fierce protectiveness, a mother's might,
A shield of love, both day and night.

Let compassion be our guiding grace,
To hold the ones we love, embrace.
Like buffalo, circling tight and strong,
We'll guard our loved ones, where they belong.

They charge as one, a thunderous beat,
A force unmatched, can't be beat.
With unwavering strength, they claim their ground,
Their purpose clear, with mighty sound.

Let conviction be our inner fire,
To stand for what is right, with heart's desire.
Like buffalo, horns held high and bright,
We'll chase our dreams, with all our might.

So take a lesson from the buffalo's might,
Be strong, resilient, stand and fight.
With watchful eyes and hearts ablaze,
We'll forge our path, through life's many maze.

American Bison

The American Buffalo, massive and grand,
A rumbling spirit across the land.
With shaggy coat and patient gaze,
He weathers storms through countless days.

Let resilience be our steadfast might,
To stand unyielding, through darkest night.

Like buffalo, strong against the gale,
We'll face adversity, and never fail.

He moves as one, with thundering stride,
In dusty herds, where strong bonds abide.
Protecting young, with fierce resolve,
A silent promise, to evolve.

Let unity be our collective power,
To stand together, in every hour.
Like buffalo, a mighty, moving force,
We'll find our strength, and stay the course.

With quiet dignity, he grazes slow,
Connected deeply to earth's ebb and flow.
No frantic rush, no needless chase,
Contentment found, in time and space.

Let groundedness root us deep and true,
To find our peace in all we do.
Like buffalo, connected to the land,
We'll find our calm, understanding's hand.

So take a lesson from the buffalo's soul,
Be strong, united, and make yourself whole.
With steadfast spirit and a peaceful stride,
You'll weather life's storms, with nothing to hide.

Water Buffalo

With massive frame and gentle eyes,
The water buffalo calmly lies.
In mud they wallow, cool and deep,
A sense of peace their slumber keeps.

Let tranquility be our guiding light,
To find our calm, and face the night.
Like water buffalo, seeking rest,
We'll find our solace, put worries to the test.

They graze in fields, a patient soul,
Contentment found, to make them whole.

With simple needs and spirits kind,
They teach us peace, of a different kind.

Let contentment be our inner wealth,
To find joy present, with mental health.
Like water buffalo, unburried by greed,
We'll find true riches, in a thankful seed.

Though powerful, they rarely fight,
Their strength lies in gentle, steady might.
With quiet resolve, they face each day,
A lesson learned, in a peaceful way.

Let inner strength be calm and sure,
To face our battles, and forever endure.
Like water buffalo, unyielding still,
We'll find our power, with gentle will.

They form a herd, a family strong,
Protecting young where they belong.
Fierce loyalty, a bond so true,
Nurturing love, forever new.

Let fierce compassion be our embrace,
To cherish loved ones, in this sacred space.
Like water buffalo, close and tight,
We'll build a haven, bathed in love's light.

So take a lesson from the gentle beast,
Be tranquil, strong, and find sweet release.
With inner peace and hearts ablaze,
We'll find our balance, through life's many maze.

5

Hoofed Mammals of Woodlands and Mountains

Deer, Reindeer, Moose, Elk,
Gray Brocket, Goat, Sheep, Ram

Deer

With eyes like pools and coat of light,
The deer leaps free, a graceful sight.
Through dappled woods and meadows green,
A gentle soul, a peaceful scene.

Let innocence be our guiding star,
To see the world, near and far.
Like deer, with hearts untouched and pure,
We'll find the beauty that can endure.

They twitch their ears and sniff the breeze,
Alert and wise, beneath the trees.

With senses keen, they navigate,
The hidden dangers, and welcome fate.

Let awareness be our guiding light,
To see the truth, with all our might.
Like deer, with senses sharp and keen,
We'll navigate life's ever-changing scene.

They gather close in herds that roam,
A sense of comfort, finding home.
With tender nudges, love they share,
A gentle bond, a loving care.

Let compassion be our guiding hand,
To understand, and truly stand.
Like deer, with hearts that softly beat,
We'll reach out kindness, and make life sweet.

So take a page from the deer's soft grace,
Be innocent, aware, embrace.
With gentle spirit, hearts alight,
We'll find our path, and walk in light.

Reindeer

With eyes like amber, coats of snow,
The reindeer prance, where blizzards blow.
Across the tundra, swift they run,
Pulling sleighs at Christmas, for everyone.

Let dedication be our guide,
To work with passion, with steady stride.
Like reindeer, pulling through the night,
We'll reach our goals, with all our might.

They dig for moss beneath the white,
With patient sniffs, a winter's right.
Through frozen ground, their noses know,
The hidden treasures, where life can grow.

Let resourcefulness be our call,
To find solutions, big or small.
Like reindeer, with senses keen,
We'll find what's needed, unseen, unseen.

In herds they gather, strong and grand,
A social bond, across the land.
They migrate together, year by year,
A family's journey, dispelling fear.

Let community be our embrace,
To build each other, with love and grace.
Like reindeer, standing side by side,
We'll face the challenges, with hearts that confide.

So take a page from the reindeer's plight,
Be dedicated, strong, and hold on tight.
With purpose clear and spirits bright,
We'll spread the joy, and make things right.

Moose

With antlers wide, a crown of bone,
The moose stands tall, a king alone.
Through tangled woods, he gracefully strides,
A gentle giant, where nature confides.

**Let strength be ours, both body and mind,
To face the world, a purpose to find.
Like moose, with muscles that ripple and flow,
We'll overcome challenges, watch our spirits grow.**

They wade in water, cool and deep,
Finding solace where secrets sleep.
With patient calm, they seek their peace,
A moment of quiet, worries to release.

Let tranquility be our guiding light,
To find stillness, and hold on tight.
Like moose, in water's gentle embrace,
We'll find our peace, in life's hurried pace.

Though solitary paths they may tread,
A loyal heart within them is bred.
For mates they fight, with fierce display,
Protecting love, in their own special way.

Let loyalty be our guiding star,
To cherish loved ones, no matter how far.
Like moose, with a bond that's strong and true,
We'll stand by our own, forever and through.

So take a page from the moose's might,
Be strong, be peaceful, hold on tight.
With gentle spirit and unwavering stride,
We'll leave our mark, with grace as our guide.

Elk

The Elk, with antlers reaching high,
A noble spirit 'neath the sky.
He roams the forests, bold and free,
A symbol of wild majesty.

Let dignity be our proud display,
To carry ourselves with grace each day.
Like elk, with heads held strong and tall,
We'll stand with purpose, answering life's call.

In bugling calls, his passion rings,
A powerful voice, a song he sings.
He vies for mates, a show of might,
Yet knows his place in forest light.

Let passion ignite our burning fire,
To strive for greatness, reaching higher.
Like elk, expressing all their will,
We'll pursue our dreams, and climb each hill.

In herds they gather, safe and sound,
Protecting yearlings on hallowed ground.
A watchful eye, a gentle nudge,
A community's strength, no one to begrudge.

Let stewardship be our guiding grace,
To guard our world, and find our place.
Like elk, protecting all they see,
We'll nurture life, for all to be.

So take a lesson from the elk's proud stride,
With dignity and passion, nothing to hide.
Protect what's precious, stand strong and true,
And let your noble spirit shine through.

Gray Brocket

The Gray Brocket, shy and small,
Through dense South American forests, he roams through all.
With cautious steps and quiet grace,
He finds his sustenance, in his hidden space.

Let humility be our gentle guide,
To walk with grace, with nothing to hide.

Like Gray Brockets, humble and serene,
We'll find our quiet strength, on life's green scene.

His senses sharp, his ears alert,
He melts into shadows, avoiding hurt.
Aware of dangers, quick to flee,
A master of evasion, wild and free.

Let awareness be our keenest sight,
To notice details, in fading light.
Like Gray Brockets, attentive and so keen,
We'll navigate challenges, on life's unseen.

Though solitary, mostly he keeps to his own,
His presence quiet, his wisdom known.
He lives in balance, with nature's flow,
A quiet life, allowing peace to grow.

Let self-reliance be our steady pace,
To find our strength, in our own space.
Like Gray Brockets, content to be,
We'll cultivate peace, for all to see.

So take a lesson from the Brocket's way,
Be humble, aware, and live each day.
With quiet strength and gentle stride,
You'll find your peace, with nothing to hide.

Goat

With nimble hooves and beard so white,
The goat ascends, a daring sight.
On rocky cliffs they pick their way,
Unafraid of heights, they love to play.

Let courage light our daring soul,
To climb the peaks and reach our goal.
Like goats, on ledges, brave and bold,
We'll face our fears, and stories unfold.

With keenest eyes, they scan the scene,
A watchful gaze, where dangers glean.

They trust their instincts, sure and wise,
And navigate, beneath the skies.

Let intuition be our guide,
To sense the path, where truth can hide.
Like goats, with wisdom all their own,
We'll find our way, when we're alone.

Though social creatures, herds they roam,
They value independence, finding their home
In rugged climbs and windy plains,
Where freedom calls, and spirit reigns.

Let independence be our call,
To forge our path, and stand up tall.
Like goats, who wander, wild and free,
We'll find our strength, eternally.

So take a cue from the goat's sure stride,
Be brave and wise, in you confide.
With hearts that yearn for open skies,
We'll reach new heights, and claim the prize.

Sheep

With coat of wool and gentle gaze,
The sheep meander, through sunlit haze.
They graze on fields, a peaceful sight,
A flock of friends, in morning light.

Let contentment be our guiding star,
To find the joy, no matter how far.
Like sheep, content with simple things,
We'll find the peace, that comfort brings.

They follow paths, well-worn and known,
A sense of trust, in what is shown.

With quiet steps and hearts at ease,
They find their comfort, in gentle breeze.

Let trust be ever in our hearts,
To follow guidance, play our parts.
Like sheep, who find their shepherd's call,
We'll trust the journey, big and small.

Though sometimes seen as meek or mild,
They gather strong, to protect their child.
A mother's love, a fierce embrace,
Defending what they love, with grace.

Let courage bloom, when shadows fall,
To stand up tall, for one and all.
Like sheep, who huddle, side by side,
We'll face the storm, with hearts that confide.

So take a page from the sheep's soft grace,
Find peace and trust, in life's embrace.
With gentle spirit, hearts content,
We'll find our way, eternally spent.

Ram

With horns held high, a stoic gaze,
The ram confronts the mountain's maze.
He scales the peaks with steady stride,
Unyielding strength, in him confide.

Let resilience be our guiding star,
Through trials climb, no matter how far.
Like rams, we'll face the uphill fight,
And reach the summit, bathed in light.

Their clashes fierce, a test of might,
Butting heads to earn their right.

Not rage, but purpose in their blows,
For leadership the victor sows.

Let competition hone our skill,
To strive for excellence, with focused will.
Like rams, we'll push ourselves to grow,
And lead the way, where knowledge can flow.

In watchful guard, the ram protects,
His flock he shelters, no rest he expects.
A duty bound, a steadfast heart,
For those he cares for, he plays his part.

Let responsibility be our vow,
To stand by others, here and now.
Like rams, we'll shield them from the storm,
And keep them safe, and ever warm.

So take a cue from the ram's bold way,
Be strong, determined, each and every day.
With purpose, focus, hearts alight,
We'll face the challenges, and make things right.

6

Primates - Our Close Relatives

*Silverback Gorilla, Chimpanzee,
Monkey, Baboon, Orangutan*

Silverback Gorilla

With massive frame and knuckles strong,
The silverback, where he belongs.
A gentle giant, wise and old,
Protects his troop, a story told.

Let strength be yours, but tempered kind,
A mighty force, with gentle mind.
Like gorillas, leaders true and bold,
Use power wisely, stories unfold.

They beat their chests, a thunderous call,
A guardian's heart, for one and all.

With watchful eyes and patient grace,
They guide their young, in every space.

Let nurturing be your guiding light,
To shelter those, and set things right.
Like gorillas, mothers strong and true,
Nurture the young, and see them through.

With playful spirit, young they roam,
Climbing and swinging, making a home.
Laughter and joy, in every beat,
A carefree dance, with tiny feet.

Let joy be ever in your heart,
Embrace the fun, and play your part.
Like gorillas, tumbling, free and bright,
Find simple pleasures, in morning light.

Though solitary paths some tread,
In family bonds, their future's read.
A social unit, strong and tight,
They face the world, with all their might.

Let community be your embrace,
To find your tribe, in every space.
Like gorillas, gathering near and far,
We build a haven, no matter who you are.

So take a page from the gorilla's might,
Be strong and gentle, hold on tight.
With purpose clear and hearts that care,
Leave paw prints deep, and love to share.

Chimpanzee

The Chimpanzee, with curious gaze,
Intelligent eyes in jungle's haze.
A tool-user, solving every plight,
With clever hands and mind so bright.

Let ingenuity be our guiding spark,
To solve problems, leaving our mark.

Like chimpanzees, inventive and wise,
We'll find new answers, beneath open skies.

In lively troops, they groom and play,
Communicating through their day.
Strong social bonds, a caring touch,
Their family ties, they cherish much.

Let community be our warm embrace,
To nurture bonds, in every space.
Like chimpanzees, connected and true,
We'll build our networks, helping me and you.

They learn from elders, watch and heed,
Passing knowledge, planting seeds.
A lifetime spent in growing skill,
Adapting always, with determined will.

Let lifelong learning fill our soul,
To seek new wisdom, making us whole.
Like chimpanzees, observing and bright,
We'll gather knowledge, with all our might.

So take a lesson from the Chimp's clever mind,
Be ingenious, communal, and truly kind.
With open heart and wisdom's quest,
You'll live your life, put to the test.

Monkey

The Monkey swings, a playful streak,
Through jungle canopies, quick and sleek.
With nimble fingers, sharp and fast,
A curious spirit, built to last.

**Let agility be our swift design,
To adapt and move, and truly shine.**

Like monkeys, lithe and full of grace,
We'll navigate life, with skillful pace.

In chattering groups, they groom and feed,
A social fabric, planting a seed.
For mutual safety, they stand as one,
Their bonds unbreakable, beneath the sun.

Let sociability brighten our day,
To connect with others, in every way.
Like monkeys, thriving in their clan,
We'll build strong friendships, a helping hand.

From branch to branch, with curious eye,
They mimic actions, reaching high.
A thirst for knowledge, an eager mind,
New ways of living, they always find.

Let inquisitiveness be our quest,
To learn and grow, putting us to the test.
Like monkeys, mirroring all they see,
We'll gather wisdom, wild and free.

So take a lesson from the monkey's zest,
Be agile, social, and put curiosity to the test.
With nimble spirit and a joyful gaze,
You'll swing through life's adventurous maze.

Baboon

The Baboon strides, with fearless gaze,
Through rocky outcrops, sun-drenched haze.
A formidable presence, strong and bold,
A story of survival, bravely told.

Let courage be our unyielding stand,
To face down challenges, across the land.

**Like baboons, unafraid and strong,
We'll stand our ground, where we belong.**

In complex troops, a hierarchy clear,
Each knows their place, dispelling fear.
With watchful eyes, they scan the plain,
For danger lurking, through sun and rain.

**Let order guide our structured way,
To find our rhythm, each and every day.
Like baboons, in their social design,
We'll seek balance, truly divine.**

They groom their kin with tender care,
A bond of comfort, shared in air.
Protecting young, with fierce embrace,
A loyalty deep, in time and space.

**Let protectiveness define our might,
To guard our loved ones, with all our light.
Like baboons, watchful and so true,
We'll shield those precious, me and you.**

*So take a lesson from the baboon's soul,
Be brave and ordered, making yourself whole.
With fierce devotion and a watchful eye,
You'll live with purpose, beneath the sky.*

Orangutan

The Orangutan, with thoughtful stare,
Through ancient forests, hangs in air.
A solitary wisdom, slow and deep,
While jungle secrets softly sleep.

Let contemplation be our inner guide,
To ponder deeply, with nothing to hide.

Like orangutans, observing the fray,
We'll seek true wisdom, lighting our way.

With patient grip, he builds his nest,
A safe retreat, a place to rest.
Resourceful hands, a gentle touch,
He asks for little, but gains so much.

Let self-sufficiency be our steady art,
To build our peace, with a tranquil heart.
Like orangutans, with careful grace,
We'll find contentment, in our own space.

Though largely solitary, a mother's embrace,
Shows tender nurture, in time and space.
Long years of teaching, soft and kind,
A lasting legacy, for those behind.

Let gentle teaching be our patient way,
To guide with love, each passing day.
Like orangutans, with wisdom shared,
We'll pass on knowledge, lovingly cared.

So take a lesson from the ape's slow grace,
Be thoughtful, self-reliant, find your peaceful space.
With quiet wisdom and a gentle hand,
You'll leave your mark upon the land.

7

Marsupials - Pouched Wonders

Kangaroo, Koala, Wombat, Quokka, Tasmanian Devil, Virginia Opossum

Kangaroo

With powerful legs and a bouncing stride,
The kangaroo hops, with the outback as guide.
A joey peeks from a pouch of delight,
A marsupial marvel, a wondrous sight.

Let freedom be yours, in every leap,
Explore your path, and dreams to keep.
Like kangaroos, on boundless plains,
Breakthrough your limits, challenge the reins.

With powerful tails for balance and grace,
They navigate steps, with nary a trace.

Strength and agility, perfectly entwined,
A symbol of resilience, for all to find.

Let adaptability be your call,
To face the changes, big and small.
Like kangaroos, in seasons dry,
Find solutions, beneath the sky.

They gather close in mobs that graze,
Sharing the bounty, in sunlit haze.
A social creature, with gentle might,
Community strong, a beautiful sight.

Let connection be your guiding hand,
To build a bond, across the land.
Like kangaroos, in huddled peace,
Find strength in love, that will never cease.

So take a page from the kangaroo's bound,
Be strong and free, on open ground.
With hearts that yearn and spirits that soar,
Leave hopping prints, forevermore.

Koala

In eucalyptus' fragrant hold,
The koala clings, a story told.
With fur of silver, eyes so round,
A gentle soul, barely a sound.

Let peacefulness be your guiding light,
Find comfort quiet, hold on tight.
Like koalas, perched in leafy ease,
Find solace soft, in nature's breeze.

They munch on leaves, a gentle sway,
Contentment found in every day.
With measured bites and watchful gaze,
They savor life, in peaceful daze.

Let mindfulness be your inner call,
To slow your pace, and give your all.
Like koalas, wise and ever true,
Live in the moment, with skies so blue.

Though solitary paths they roam,
A mother's love, protects their home.
With watchful care, they raise their young,
A gentle bond, where hearts are sung.

Let loyalty be your guiding hand,
To cherish those, in shifting sand.
Like koalas, close in furry hold,
Love fiercely deep, a story told.

But threats arise, their numbers shrink,
Habitat lost, on forest's brink.
Let's protect their world, with gentle might,
The koalas, slumbering, day and night.

So take a page from the koala's grace,
Find peace and love, in nature's embrace.
With gentle spirit and heart's soft beat,
Live simply kind, forever sweet.

Wombat

A burrower bold, with fur of brown,
The wombat waddles, a sturdy clown.
Short legs and claws for digging deep,
In tunnels cool, secrets they keep.

Let resilience be your guiding light,
To weather storms and hold on tight.
Like wombats strong, in earth they hide,
Find inner strength, where dangers reside.

They munch on grasses, green and sweet,
With powerful jaws, a vegetarian feat.
Contentment found in simple fare,
A happy heart, without a care.

Let peacefulness be your guiding hand,
Find joy in moments, close at hand.
Like wombats, grazing through the day,
Savor life's bounty, come what may.

Though solitary paths they roam,
A watchful eye protects their home.
With fierce defense, for young they fight,
A love that burns, eternally bright.

Let loyalty be your guiding hand,
To stand by loved ones, in shifting sand.
Like wombats, fierce when danger calls,
Protect your pack, and stand up tall.

A curious soul, with nose that sniffs,
They sniff out danger, with clever shifts.
Adaptability, their secret key,
Thriving in nature's symphony.

Let resourcefulness be your call,
To find solutions, big and small.
Like wombats, with minds so keen,
Solve life's puzzles, on the scene.

So take a cue from the wombat's might,
Be strong, content, and hold on tight.
With purpose clear and heart at ease,
Dig deep your dreams, beneath the trees.

Quokka

With eyes so bright and grin so wide,
The quokka hops, with joyful stride.
A ball of sunshine, fur a dusty grey,
They munch on leaves, and brighten your day.

Let happiness be your guiding light,
Spread joy and warmth, with all your might.
Like quokkas, smiling through and through,
Infect the world, with sunshine true.

Though shy and gentle, with twitching nose,
They watch the world, from hidden rose.
Contentment found, in simple fare,
A peaceful spirit, beyond compare.

Let mindfulness be your inner call,
To find the beauty, big and small.
Like quokkas, pausing in the sun,
Savor the moment, 'til the day is done.

Though solitary paths they roam,
For joeys loved, they make a home.
With watchful care, they nurture young,
A love that blossoms, clear and strong.

Let nurturing be your guiding hand,
To cherish those in shifting sand.
Like quokkas, gentle, kind, and true,
Protect your loved ones, forever new.

But threats arise, their numbers shrink,
Habitat loss, on forest's brink.
Let's mend the harm, and set them free,
The quokkas smiling, eternally.

So take a page from the quokka's glee,
Be happy, gentle, and forever free.
With hearts that brim and spirits bright,
Spread sunshine's warmth, with all your might.

Tasmanian Devil

The Tasmanian Devil, fierce and bold,
A stocky fighter, stories told.
With powerful jaws and rasping growl,
He faces challenges, chasing down a foul.

Let tenacity be our stubborn will,
To hold our ground, and stand quite still.

Like devils, holding on so tight,
We'll fight for what's true, with all our might.

A scavenger, making waste his fare,
No opportunity lost, beyond compare.
Resourceful spirit, rugged and keen,
Thriving in wilds, a wild-eyed scene.

Let resourcefulness guide our way,
To make the most of every day.
Like devils, finding what they need,
We'll sow good outcomes, planting every seed.

Though solitary often, when food is found,
A cacophony erupts on hallowed ground.
Social at times, a fierce display,
Then back to solitude, come what may.

Let fierce independence be our core,
To walk our path, and ask for more.
Like devils, strong when standing alone,
We'll chart our course, truly our own.

So take a lesson from the devil's might,
Be tenacious, resourceful, and fiercely bright.
With stubborn courage and a wild heart's quest,
You'll put your true self to the test.

Virginia Opossum

The Virginia Opossum, slow and shy,
A nocturnal wanderer 'neath the sky.
With grasping tail and pouch so deep,
Secrets of survival, he will keep.

**Let adaptability be our gentle art,
To make the most of every part.**

Like opossums, finding their way,
We'll thrive in changes, come what may.

When danger threatens, he plays quite dead,
A clever tactic, fear instead.
A master of deception, truly grand,
Outsmarting foes across the land.

Let cleverness be our thinking mind,
To find smart solutions, one of a kind.
Like opossums, wise and keen,
We'll navigate troubles, on life's tough scene.

A mother's pouch, a haven warm,
Protecting young from every storm.
With tender care, she guides her brood,
A selfless love, misunderstood.

Let nurturing be our open heart,
To shield and cherish, playing our part.
Like opossums, devoted and true,
We'll guard our loved ones, me and you.

So take a lesson from the opossum's grace,
Be adaptable, clever, find your peaceful space.
With thoughtful wisdom and a caring hand,
You'll journey safely across the land.

8

Rodents and Small Mammals

*Squirrel, Chipmunk, Mouse, Capybara,
Beaver, Raccoon, Meerkat, Sloth*

Squirrel

The busy squirrel, darting quick,
With bushy tail and acrobatic trick.
A blur of motion, up and down,
Gathering treasures, scattered all around.

Let resourcefulness be our guide,
No time to waste, with nowhere to hide.
Like squirrels, nimble, sharp, and keen,
We'll find solutions, where none are seen.

They bury nuts for winter's chill,
A plan for future, with practiced skill.
Remembering stashes, hidden tight,
Prepared for hardship, with all their might.

Let foresight be our guiding star,
To plan for challenges, no matter how far.
Like squirrels, we'll think ahead and store,
For future needs, and nothing more.

In playful chases, tails held high,
They chase and frolic, beneath the sky.
A zest for life, a joyful dance,
Finding amusement in every chance.

Let playfulness lighten our way,
Embrace the joy in each and every day.
Like squirrels, with hearts so free,
We'll find the fun, for all to see.

Though solitary some may roam,
They share their knowledge, make a forest home.
Alarms they sound, a warning cry,
Protecting all, beneath the watchful sky.

Let community be our guiding light,
To lend a hand, and make things right.
Like squirrels, united, strong, and bold,
We'll build a world, where stories unfold.

So take a cue from the squirrel's might,
Be clever, plan, and find delight.
With playful spirit, hearts ablaze,
We'll gather wisdom through life's many maze.

Chipmunk

The chipmunk scurries, quick and bright,
With stripes of brown and fur so light.
Cheek pouches full, a hurried dash,
Gathering bounty in a playful flash.

Let industriousness be our guide,
With tireless effort, take life in stride.
Like chipmunks, busy, never slow,
We'll plant the seeds that help us grow.

They gather treasures, big and small,
Nuts and seeds to answer winter's call.
A constant hustle, a driven soul,
Preparing for the future, making them whole.

Let perseverance be our inner strength,
Through challenges faced, at any length.
Like chipmunks, persistent, never quit,
We'll reach our goals, with focused grit.

Their chatters fill the air with glee,
A joyful spirit, wild and free.
They play and frolic, hearts alight,
Finding amusement in morning's light.

Let optimism be our guiding ray,
Embrace the sunshine, chase the gray.
Like chipmunks, cheerful, full of song,
We'll find the joy where we belong.

Though small in stature, voices strong,
They warn of danger, righting any wrong.
A watchful eye, a loyal friend,
Protecting all until the very end.

Let vigilance be our watchword true,
For those we care for, me and you.
Like chipmunks, guarding, ever keen,
We'll stand by others, on life's sharp scene.

So take a lesson from the chipmunk's dash,
Be hardworking, cheerful, in a joyful flash.
With focused spirit, hearts alight,
We'll fill our lives with purpose bright.

Mouse

The tiny mouse, a scurrying sight,
In walls they dwell, beneath the night.
With whiskered nose and senses keen,
They navigate the unseen scene.

Let curiosity be our guide,
To explore and learn, with mind open wide.
Like mice, we'll delve in questions deep,
And seek out knowledge, secrets to keep.

They scavenge scraps with clever mind,
From giants' feasts, what they can find.
Resourceful hearts, they waste no part,
Making the most with a thrifty art.

Let adaptability be our might,
To find solutions, in day and night.
Like mice, we'll bend and never break,
And thrive in challenges, for goodness sake.

Though small and unseen, they build their home,
A network vast, where they safely roam.
Together strong, a social band,
They face the world, paw in tiny hand.

Let cooperation be our call,
To work together, and stand up tall.
Like mice, united, heart to heart,
We'll build a world where no one falls apart.

So take a hint from the mouse so small,
Be curious, clever, and answer life's call.
With teamwork strong and a mind to explore,
We'll find our way, forevermore.

Capybara

A hippo's charm, a guinea pig's grin,
The capybara waddles, a gentle kin.
Semi-aquatic, a social delight,
King of the marsh, with fur soft and bright.

Let peacefulness be your guiding light,
Embrace the calm, with all your might.
Like capybaras, lounging in the sun,
Find joy in stillness, 'til the day is done.

They graze on grasses, in groups they roam,
A network of friends, wherever they go.

Sharing the bounty, with trust and with cheer,
Harmony reigns, year after year.

Let community be your guiding hand,
Build bridges strong, across the land.
Like capybaras, no one left behind,
In friendships true, a solace you'll find.

Though danger lurks, from predators bold,
Alerts they sound, a story told.
With watchful eyes and powerful swim,
They find their haven, safe within.

Let vigilance guide you, ever keen,
Be prepared and focused, on what's unseen.
Like capybaras, aware and wise,
Face challenges, with brave, clear eyes.

From caiman's bite to jaguar's prowl,
They share their space, with nature's whole howl.
A gentle giant, in a world so grand,
The capybara, a peaceful stand.

So take a cue from the capybara's grace,
Be calm, be kind, and find your space.
With gentle spirit and heart alight,
Spread peace and joy, with all your might.

Beaver

With orange teeth and tireless paws,
The beaver builds, defying laws.
They gnaw on wood, a constant hum,
Architects of nature's kingdom.

Let diligence be our guiding light,
To work with purpose, day and night.
Like beavers, toiling with such might,
We'll craft our goals, and make them right.

With dams they channel, waters flow,
A web of life, where creatures grow.
They change their world, with every bite,
Reshaping landscapes, shining bright.

Let innovation be our keenest tool,
To find new paths, and break each rule.
Like beavers, ever curious and bold,
We'll solve life's puzzles, stories unfold.

In lodges built with mud and stick,
Families gather, strong and thick.
They share their work, their food, their space,
A bond of teamwork, leaving no trace.

Let collaboration be our guiding hand,
To build together, make a stand.
Like beavers, united, purpose clear,
We'll reach new heights, conquer any fear.

So take a lesson from the beaver's might,
Be diligent, inventive, hold on tight.
With steady work and hearts that care,
We'll build a world, both strong and fair.

Raccoon

With mask of black and bandit eyes,
The raccoon creeps, a sly surprise.
A ringed tail swishes, a curious nose,
n trash cans rummaging, where mischief grows.

Let cunning guide you, wise and keen,
To find your bounty, unseen, unseen.
Like raccoons, with paws so quick,
Uncover treasures, with a playful trick.

They scamper nimbly, through moonlit night,
Acrobatic souls, a playful might.
On branches high, they balance grand,
Masters of movement, across the land.

Let adaptability be your call,
To climb and bend, and weather all.
Like raccoons, clever and light,
Find solutions, in darkest night.

With curious paws, they explore and touch,
The world's a puzzle, to love so much.
A playful spirit, a heart that seeks,
Adventure's call, in rustling creeks.

Let inquisitiveness be your guide,
To ask and wonder, with open wide.
Like raccoons, with boundless quest,
Unravel mysteries, put life to the test.

(Though some may find them quite a plight,
These masked bandits, stealing through the night,
They hold a charm, a curious grace,
A touch of mischief, in nature's embrace.)

So take a cue from the raccoon's might,
Be clever, nimble, and hold on tight.
With playful spirit and curious paws,
Explore the world, forever because.

Meerkat

With watchful eyes and standing tall,
The meerkat surveys, guarding all.
A social soul, in burrowed home,
They work as one, where none feel alone.

Let cooperation be our key,
To build together, you and me.
Like meerkats, sharing sun and sand,
We'll raise a village, hand in hand.

They stand on guard, a watchful eye,
While others forage, 'neath the sky.

With selfless acts, they play their part,
A caring spirit, from the start.

Let empathy be our guiding light,
To see through others', day and night.
Like meerkats, standing tall and true,
We'll feel their joys and sorrows too.

The young they nurture, safe and warm,
A loving bond that weathers storm.
With fierce devotion, hearts ablaze,
They raise their pups through playful days.

Let nurturing be our gentle touch,
To guide the young, and love them much.
Like meerkats, patient, kind, and strong,
We'll help them grow, where they belong.

Though small in stature, bold and bright,
They face the dangers, day and night.
With constant watch and warning call,
They stand united, through it all.

Let vigilance be our inner shield,
To guard our dreams, what we hold revealed.
Like meerkats, ever on the lookout,
We'll face our fears, and have no doubt.

So take a lesson from the meerkat band,
Work together, heart and hand.
With watchful eyes and spirits strong,
We'll build a world, where we all belong.

Sloth

With upside-down grin and leisurely pace,
The sloth hangs languid, a master of space.
Three-toed grip on branches so high,
A silent observer, with moss in its eye.

Let slowness guide you, a mindful refrain,
Savor the journey, not just the gain.
Like sloths, suspended in verdant embrace,
Find inner peace, with a deliberate pace.

They munch on leaves, a methodical feat,
Conserving energy, a nature-taught cheat.

Less haste, less stress, a wisdom untold,
Simple contentment, more precious than gold.

Let patience be your guiding light,
Wait and observe, with all your might.
Like sloths, hanging tight through the day,
Wisdom unfolds, in its own patient way.

Though seemingly still, they traverse with care,
A hidden agility, a secret to share.
Underneath fur, slow muscles reside,
Steady and sure, with a silent stride.

Let determination be your call,
Move at your pace, and conquer it all.
Like sloths, persistent, unseen yet so bold,
Reach for your goals, with stories untold.

(Habitat loss, a threat to their kind,
Rainforests receding, leaving them behind.
Let's protect their haven, from the ground to the trees,
For the gentle sloth, forever at ease.)

So take a page from the sloth's gentle might,
Be slow and mindful, hold on tight.
With tranquil spirit and patient embrace,
Find your own rhythm, in nature's sweet space.

9

Marine Mammals - Life in the Water

Seal, Walrus, Bottlenose Dolphin, Orca

Seal

With sleek, grey fur and eyes so bright,
The seal emerges, a playful sight.
On land they flop, in clumsy grace,
But dive in water, with nary a trace.

Let adaptability be our guide,
To thrive on land, and ocean's tide.
Like seals, we'll navigate with ease,
Through life's all aspects, finding peace.

They bask in sun, a blubbery bunch,
Contentment found, with playful hunch.
They rest and recharge, for dives below,
A balance struck, where pleasures flow.

Let self-care be our guiding star,
To nourish minds and bodies, no matter how far.
Like seals, who take their moments true,
We'll find our rest, and start anew.

They gather close, in colonies strong,
Pups nuzzle mothers, where they belong.
A social bond, a loving crew,
They nurture young, with hearts so true.

Let community be our embrace,
To find our tribe, in every space.
Like seals, who huddle, warm and near,
We'll build connections, precious and dear.

With barks and whistles, they fill the air,
A symphony shared, a joyful flair.
They communicate, with playful glee,
A vibrant chorus, for all to see.

Let connection be our purpose true,
To bridge the gaps, for me and you.
Like seals, who call across the waves,
We'll share our voices, strong and brave.

So take a page from the seal's delight,
Be flexible, find joy, and hold on tight.
With open hearts and playful soul,
We'll navigate life, making us whole.

Walrus

With wrinkled hide and tusks of bone,
The walrus waddles, never alone.
Her gruff pronouncements fill the air,
A social giant, with a walrus stare.

Let resilience be our guiding light,
To weather storms, and hold on tight.
Like walruses, on icy floes,
We'll face the challenges, life bestows.

They huddle close, a massive herd,
A fortress built, each word unheard.
For warmth and safety, side by side,
They face the north, with stoic pride.

Let community be our embrace,
To find our tribe, in every space.
Like walruses, with tusks held high,
We'll stand together, reach for the sky.

They use their tusks to break the ice,
And dig for clams, a tasty slice.
Persistent hunters, strong and bold,
They find their bounty, stories unfold.

Let resourcefulness be our guide,
To find our way, with hearts inside.
Like walruses, with whiskers keen,
We'll seek our goals, unseen, unheard, unseen.

So take a page from the walrus' might,
Be strong, be loud, and hold on tight.
With skin so thick and hearts of gold,
We'll face the world, brave and bold.

Bottlenose Dolphin

With bodies sleek and minds so keen,
The bottlenose dolphins, a playful scene.
They leap and twist, a flash of grey,
Acrobatic wonders in ocean's spray.

Let joy be yours, a constant tide,
In laughter's dance, where worries hide.
Like dolphins, playful, hearts alight,
Embrace the fun, with all your might.

Their whistles echo, a language deep,
Secrets they share, in the ocean's keep.
With clicks and chirps, they navigate,
A social network, where love won't abate.

Let communication be your guide,
To bridge the gaps, with openness inside.
Like dolphins, sharing stories untold,
Connect and learn, with young and old.

They hunt in pods, with teamwork strong,
Herding their prey, where they all belong.
Cooperation's key, a lesson wise,
Together they thrive, beneath the skies.

Let unity be your guiding star,
To work together, however far.
Like dolphins, swimming side by side,
Reach for your goals, in joyful stride.

(But tangled nets and changing seas,
Threaten their dance, with sorrow's breeze.
Let's protect their world, forever vast,
For dolphins, playful, meant to last.)

So take a cue from the dolphin's grace,
Be joyful, wise, and find your place.
With hearts that sing and spirits bold,
Leave trails of wonder, stories unfold.

Orca

With sleek black form and piercing eye,
The orca glides, beneath the sky.
A flash of white, a dorsal fin,
The ocean's hunter, swift within.

Let power grace your every stride,
A force of nature, deep inside.
Like orcas, strong and bold and wise,
Command respect, with knowing eyes.

They echolocate, a haunting sound,
Through ocean depths, their secrets found.

Communication, a complex art,
A language shared, that warms the heart.

Let wisdom be your guiding light,
To speak your truth, with all your might.
Like orcas, voices in the sea,
Let your message flow, eternally.

In family pods, they hunt and roam,
A matriarch leads, to bring them home.
With fierce protection, young they tend,
A loyal bond, that knows no end.

Let family be your guiding hand,
To cherish those in shifting sand.
Like orcas, close in every way,
Find strength in love, and brighter day.

(Though painted villain, misunderstood,
They keep the balance, ocean's good.
Let's protect their world, and set them free,
The orcas sing, eternally.)

So take a cue from the orca's might,
Be strong and wise, and hold on tight.
With purpose clear and family near,
Glide through life, with hearts that hold you dear.

10

Reptiles - Scales and Shells

Crocodile, Alligator, Komodo Dragon,

King Cobra, Iguana, Lizard, Tortoise,
Painted Turtle

Crocodile

The crocodile, in murky depths unseen,
A silent hunter, patient, and serene.
With eyes that gleam and ancient might,
He waits for prey, with stealthy sight.

Let focus be our guiding light,
To hone our skills and see things right.
Like crocodiles, we'll train our gaze,
And chase our goals through focused days.

Their powerful jaws, a fearsome clamp,
Once gripped, escape's a fading lamp.
Persistence guides them, never quit,
Until their target's firmly hit.

Let tenacity be our inner drive,
To never falter, never give in strive.
Like crocodiles, we'll hold on tight,
And see our dreams emerge to light.

Though danger lurks beneath the wave,
They bring stability, the ecosystem they save.
A vital cog, in nature's grand design,
Their presence keeps the balance fine.

Let responsibility be our call,
To play our part, for one and all.
Like crocodiles, maintain the flow,
Upholding balance, where we grow.

However, caution with their power blends,
Unprovoked attacks, where danger transcends.
Let wisdom guide the strength we hold,
For measured action, worth more than gold.

Let wisdom be the tempering rain,
On power's fire, to ease the strain.
Like crocodiles, with measured might,
We'll use our strength to make things right.

So take a page from the croc's domain,
Be focused, strong, a force to sustain.
With mindful action, wisdom's grace,
We'll leave our mark on this earthly space.

Alligator

The gator lurks, a patient might,
In swampy depths, where shadows fight.
With armored hide and toothy grin,
A primal power resides within.

Let resilience be our guiding force,
To weather storms and chart a course.
Like alligators, tough and strong,
We'll rise from setbacks, right any wrong.

They burst from water, swift and bold,
Claws sharp and fierce, a story told.
But measured strikes, not random rage,
Secure their prey from nature's stage.

Let strategy be wisdom's call,
To plan with foresight, conquer all.
Like alligators, cunning and keen,
We'll choose our battles, where success is seen.

Though solitary hunters they roam,
For mates they bellow, call back home.
A fierce display of primal sound,
A love expressed, on sacred ground.

Let passion ignite our spirits bright,
For causes true, with all our might.
Like alligators, bold and loud,
We'll fight for what we believe, uncowed.

So take a page from the gator's might,
Be tough, be clever, and fight for what's right.
With strength and passion, hearts ablaze,
We'll carve our path through life's ever-changing maze.

Komodo Dragon

The Komodo dragon, island lord,
A fearsome sight, with scales adorned.
A patient hunter, senses keen,
Scavenger king, a silent scene.

Let resourcefulness be our guide,
From scraps and waste, new things confide.
Like Komodo dragons, keen and bright,
We'll find new uses, in fading light.

Their forked tongue flickers, tasting air,
Unearthing secrets, hidden there.
Adept at sensing what lies ahead,
Intuition strong, where others tread.

Let intuition be our inner map,
To navigate with a knowing tap.
Like Komodo dragons, wise and old,
We'll trust our gut, a story told.

Though solitary most of their days,
Mating battles erupt in a fiery haze.
For dominance they fight and strive,
A dance of power to keep alive.

Let competition build us strong,
To push our limits, where we belong.
Like Komodo dragons, fierce and bold,
We'll rise to challenges, stories unfold.

Their venom potent, a deadly surprise,
A single bite, and the victim dies.
But targeted strikes, a measured sting,
Not reckless fury, victory they bring.

Let control be our guiding hand,
To wield our power across the land.
Like Komodo dragons, potent and true,
We'll use our strength, in all we do.

So take a lesson from the dragon's might,
Be resourceful, wise, and use your fight.
With keen instincts and power held tight,
We'll conquer challenges, and claim our light.

King Cobra

The king cobra rears, a hooded might,
Scales gleaming black in sunlit light.
A serpent king, with venom's touch,
His every move demands so much.

Let focus be our guiding light,
To sharpen skills with all our might.
Like king cobras, with gaze intense,
We'll train our minds for excellence.

He strikes with speed, a deadly blow,
But only threatened, never quick to go
On needless hunts. His power's held tight,
Used with precision, day and night.

Let control be our inner strength,
To channel passion, use it at length.
Like king cobras, calm and keen,
We'll find our power, where it's truly seen.

Though solitary most days he spends,
A watchful guard, his family defends.
For mates he dances, a threatening sway,
A fierce display to chase all threats away.

Let loyalty be fierce and bright,
For those we cherish, with all our might.
Like king cobras, with love untold,
We'll guard our loved ones, brave and bold.

So take a lesson from the cobra's might,
Be focused, strong, and use your fight.
With measured power and hearts ablaze,
We'll face life's challenges through life's many maze.

Iguana

With scales like armor, green and grand,
The iguana basks, a spiky band.
On sun-warmed rocks, they stretch and preen,
A prehistoric king, a regal scene.

Let confidence be your guiding light,
Embrace your strength, with all your might.
Like iguanas, perched upon a throne,
Own your power, and make it known.

Their watchful eyes scan leafy greens,
A vegetarian feast, on jungle scenes.

With powerful jaws and tongue so quick,
They munch on leaves, with every flick.

Let resourcefulness be your call,
To find solutions, big and small.
Like iguanas, with a taste for green,
Find sustenance, on nature's scene.

Though solitary paths they roam,
For mates they fight, to find a home.
With bobbing heads and dewlaps bright,
They claim their love, in morning light.

Let passion guide you, strong and true,
Fight for what's yours, in shades of blue.
Like iguanas, with colors bold,
Show your true self, stories untold.

(Though habitat loss casts a threat,
Forests shrinking, a rising fret.
Let's protect their haven, wild and grand,
The iguanas, scaly kings of the land.)

So take a page from the iguana's might,
Be bold and strong, and hold on tight.
With spiky armor and hearts set free,
Leave lasting prints, eternally.

Lizard

A flicker of scales, a flash of green,
The lizard darts, a sunlit scene.
Across the rocks, a nimble stride,
A tiny hunter, with eyes so wide.

Let curiosity be your guiding light,
Explore the world, with all your might.
Like lizards, basking, ever keen,
Uncover secrets, yet unseen.

Their tongues dart out, to taste the air,
A flick of pink, a cautious flare.

With senses sharp, they sense their prize,
A hidden insect, a sweet surprise.

Let awareness be your mindful art,
To see beyond, and play your part.
Like lizards, watching, quick and bright,
Discern the truth, in fading light.

Though small they seem, in nature's grand design,
A vital role, in web that entwine.
They keep bugs in check, a balanced scheme,
A silent hero, in nature's dream.

Let respect be yours, for all that thrives,
From smallest creatures, to towering hives.
Like lizards, sharing sun and stone,
Find harmony, where all are known.

So take a cue from the lizard's might,
Be curious, quick, and hold on tight.
With watchful eyes and hearts so bold,
Leave tiny tracks, in stories untold.

Tortoise

The tortoise plods, a patient soul,
With steady steps that reach their goal.
No frantic rush, no fleeting chase,
He carries on with steady pace.

Let perseverance be our guide,
Through slow pursuits, where dreams reside.
Like tortoises, we'll take our time,
And build success, one step at a time.

Beneath his shell, a world unseen,
A quiet strength, a wisdom keen.

He carries burdens, light or grand,
Unfazed by troubles in the sand.

Let inner peace be our domain,
A calm resolve, through sun or rain.
Like tortoises, we'll find our core,
And weather storms that rage and roar.

He lives a life of measured tread,
Contentment found in what is said.
No need for haste, no restless quest,
He finds his joy in simple rest.

Let mindfulness be ever near,
To savor moments, hold them dear.
Like tortoises, we'll learn to be,
Present and grateful, eternally.

So take a lesson from the shell's embrace,
Be patient, wise, and find your space.
With steady steps and tranquil mind,
A tortoise's life, true peace we'll find.

Painted Turtle

With stripes of red and yellow bright,
The painted turtle, a dazzling sight.
In sunlit shallows, glides with ease,
A splash of joy on gentle breeze.

Let optimism be our guiding ray,
Find beauty's spark, in every day.
Like painted turtles, vibrant hue,
Let's chase the joy, the whole world through.

Though shells may shield from dangers near,
They share their space, with naught to fear.

Community strong, a vibrant web,
Together thriving, where life is bred.

Let connection be our open door,
Embrace our neighbors, evermore.
Like painted turtles, basking side by side,
In shared sunshine, let kindness confide.

From pond to shore, they make their way,
Adapting well, come what may.
Through changing seasons, ever keen,
They thrive in balance, a vibrant scene.

Let resilience be our inner tide,
With changing currents, learn to ride.
Like painted turtles, bend but don't break,
Find strength within, for fortune's sake.

So take a page from the painted one's plight,
Be joyful, connected, and hold on tight.
With vibrant spirit, and heart alight,
We'll paint our world, ever hopeful and bright.

11 | Amphibians - Life Between Water and Land

Toad, Salamander, Frog, Newt,

Axolotl, Caecilian, Mudpuppy, Hellbender

Toad

Let resilience be our guiding star,
Through changing seasons, no matter how far.
Like toads, we'll adapt to all we face,
Transforming challenges with enduring grace.

They hide in burrows, safe and deep,
Emerging gladly when the warm rains seep.
Aestivating slumber, a patient wait,
For life's renewal, to celebrate.

Let patience be our virtue true,
Knowing some things take time to accrue.
Like toads, we'll trust in the coming spring,
And with each setback, new solutions bring.

Their sticky tongues unfurl with might,
Snapping up insects in the fading light.
Ambush predators, with sights set keen,
They find their bounty, unseen, unheard, serene.

Let resourcefulness be our guide,
With creativity, where solutions hide.
Like toads, we'll find unexpected ways,
To overcome hurdles, and brighten our days.

Though some may find them slimy and slow,
They play a vital role, as nature's flow.
Mosquito eaters, keeping things in check,
A silent hero, with a valuable speck.

Let purpose guide us on our way,
To find our niche, and brighten the day.
Like toads, we all have a role to play,
Big or small, to make things okay.

So take a cue from the toad's humble might,
Be adaptable, patient, and find your light.
With resourceful spirit and purpose true,
We'll hop through life, with much to do.

Salamander

With skin of fire, a flickering spark,
The salamander leaves its slimy mark.
In damp retreats, where shadows creep,
A wriggling wonder, secrets to keep.

Let adaptability be your guide,
In shifting waters, find your stride.
Like salamanders, changing form with ease,
Embrace the flow, on life's wild seas.

Their lungs may breathe, their gills may take,
Survival's dance, for life's sweet sake.

On land they wander, or in water hide,
Masters of both, where secrets reside.

Let resourcefulness be your call,
To find solutions, big and small.
Like salamanders, thriving everywhere,
Adapt and prosper, with mindful care.

With fiery hues, a warning bright,
They ward off danger, in fading light.
A hidden power, in colors bold,
A story whispered, yet to be told.

Let inner strength be your guiding hand,
To face your fears, in shifting sand.
Like salamanders, bold and bright,
Shine from within, with all your might.

(But wetlands shrink, their habitat wanes,
Pollution's grip, a web of chains.
Let's protect their haven, cool and clear,
The salamanders, forever hold dear.)

So take a page from the salamander's might,
Be bold, adaptable, hold on tight.
With fiery spirit and heart set free,
Leave shimmering trails, eternally.

Frog

The Frog, a marvel, sleek and green,
A leaping hunter, rarely seen.
From tadpole days to croaking night,
He calls for rain, with all his might.

**Let transformation be our inner quest,
To grow and change, putting us to the test.**

Like frogs, embracing every stage,
We'll turn each leaf, on life's wide page.

With sticky tongue, he snags his prey,
A sudden strike, throughout the day.
Patiently waiting, eyes alert,
He seizes chances, avoiding hurt.

Let opportunism guide our hand,
To grasp good moments, across the land.
Like frogs, swift and keenly aware,
We'll seize our chances, beyond compare.

In damp retreats, with others near,
Their chorus rises, loud and clear.
A vibrant symphony, a common sound,
Life thriving richly, on wet, fertile ground.

Let community be our harmonious plea,
To sing together, for all to see.
Like frogs, in chorus, strong and bold,
We'll share our lives, stories untold.

So take a lesson from the frog's quick leap,
Embrace your changes, secrets to keep.
With ready spirit and a joyful sound,
You'll find your purpose, on hallowed ground.

Newt

The Newt, in ponds, a creature small,
Through water gliding, answering nature's call.
With gentle movements, slow and deep,
Secrets of the wetlands, he does keep.

Let adaptability be our soft embrace,
To thrive in change, with quiet grace.

Like newts, transitioning, sleek and keen,
We'll find our comfort, on life's ever-changing scene.

He regenerates, a wondrous art,
Regrowing limbs, a brand new start.
Resilience flows within his vein,
Overcoming setbacks, again and again.

Let resilience be our inner strength,
To heal from wounds, at any length.
Like newts, renewing, whole and bright,
We'll mend our spirits, with all our might.

In quiet corners, he finds his peace,
A solitary world, where worries cease.
Observing life, with ancient eye,
Beneath the moss, beneath the sky.

Let contemplation be our thoughtful gaze,
To find calm moments, in life's busy maze.
Like newts, observing, still and low,
We'll gather wisdom, watch our spirits grow.

So take a lesson from the newt's soft way,
Be adaptable, resilient, each and every day.
With quiet wisdom and a healing art,
You'll navigate life, with a steadfast heart.

Axolotl

The Axolotl, with frilled, gentle face,
A timeless wonder, in watery space.
Forever young, in liquid grace he lies,
A neotenic beauty, beneath tranquil skies.

Let perpetual youth be our inner glow,
To hold onto wonder, and help spirits grow.

Like axolotls, fresh and ever new,
We'll keep curiosity, in all that we do.

With power to heal, a wondrous feat,
Regrowing limbs, making life complete.
From every wound, a strength renewed,
A living testament, understood.

Let regeneration be our healing art,
To mend our spirits, and play a new part.
Like axolotls, restoring what's lost,
We'll rise from challenges, counting the cost.

Though simple seeming, a unique design,
In placid waters, their true selves shine.
They thrive in stillness, a gentle flow,
Finding contentment, wherever they go.

Let authenticity be our gentle truth,
To be truly ourselves, from age to youth.
Like axolotls, unique and so rare,
We'll embrace our true nature, beyond compare.

So take a lesson from the axolotl's calm,
Embrace renewal, safe from all harm.
With youthful spirit and a healing soul,
You'll live your life, making yourself whole.

Caecilian

The Caecilian, unseen and deep,
Through hidden tunnels, secrets to keep.
A legless wonder, sleek and profound,
Navigating darkness, beneath the ground.

**Let introspection be our inner quest,
To delve within, and put our minds to the test.**

Like caecilians, in their hidden might,
We'll find deep wisdom, away from the light.

With senses sharp, in earth they glide,
Feeling vibrations, where true paths hide.
No need for eyes, in shadowed domain,
They trust their instincts, through sun and rain.

Let intuition be our guiding sense,
To trust our gut, with no pretense.
Like caecilians, feeling their way along,
We'll find our direction, where we belong.

They guard their young with fierce embrace,
Coiled around eggs, in a hidden space.
A mother's devotion, profound and deep,
A silent promise, she will keep.

Let protectiveness be our loving care,
To shield our precious, beyond compare.
Like caecilians, nurturing and true,
We'll guard our loved ones, me and you.

So take a lesson from the caecilian's plight,
Be introspective, trust your inner light.
With quiet wisdom and a loving heart,
You'll play your unique, essential part.

Mudpuppy

The Mudpuppy, in waters deep and cold,
A salamander's secret, ages old.
With feathery gills, a permanent display,
He breathes the currents, day by day.

Let steadfastness be our constant grace,
To hold our ground, in time and space.
Like mudpuppies, rooted and so true,
We'll stand firm always, in all that we do.

Beneath the rocks, he finds his quiet lair,
A hidden life, beyond compare. Content
with stillness, rarely seen,
A master of patience, serene.

Let contentment be our inner peace,
To find calm moments, where worries cease.
Like mudpuppies, tranquil and so still,
We'll seek out quiet, bending to our will.

Through changing seasons, he persists and thrives,
A simple existence, where true life thrives.
Unbothered by surface, he knows his place,
A silent wisdom, in nature's embrace.

Let resilience be our steady heart,
To overcome trials, playing our part.
Like mudpuppies, enduring and strong,
We'll navigate challenges, where we belong.

So take a lesson from the mudpuppy's quiet way,
Be steadfast, content, through every day.
With tranquil spirit and a resilient soul,
You'll find your purpose, making yourself whole.

Hellbender

The Hellbender, giant of the stream,
A camouflaged master, like a living dream.
Flat and broad, he grips the stone,
A silent guardian, on his river throne.

Let groundedness be our steady core,
To hold our place, and ask for more.
Like Hellbenders, firm against the flow,
We'll stand our ground, and help ourselves grow.

With wrinkled skin, absorbing life,
He breathes the current, avoiding strife.
A slow, deliberate, ancient being,
Patiently waiting, for what's fleeting.

Let patience be our timeless art,
To wait for moments, playing our part.
Like Hellbenders, still and always deep,
We'll learn life's rhythms, secrets to keep.

Beneath the rocks, he makes his home,
A hidden world, where he can roam.
Guarding his eggs, a fierce display,
Protecting future, come what may.

Let stewardship guide our gentle hand,
To care for others, across the land.
Like Hellbenders, nurturing and true,
We'll shield our world, for me and you.

So take a lesson from the Hellbender's might,
Be grounded, patient, and do what is right.
With steadfast spirit and a watchful soul,
You'll play your part, making the world whole.

12

Birds of Prey

Eagle, Owl, Hawk, Secretarybird,

Osprey, Baza, Kite, Buzzard, Vulture

Eagle

With piercing gaze and wings unbound,
The eagle soars, where few are found.
Above the clouds, a lonely king,
A heart of freedom, on the wind he'll swing.

Let independence be our guiding star,
To chart our course, however far.
Like eagles, soaring on their own,
We'll find our strength, and make it known.

He spots his prey from distant sight,
A keen observer, taking flight.

With focused mind and sharpened beak,
He claims his prize, without a squeak.

Let focus be our mindful art,
To see the goal, and play our part.
Like eagles, with vision clear and true,
We'll chase our dreams, and see them through.

Though solitary in his reign,
He shares his aerie, sun and rain.
With watchful mate and loyal brood,
He builds a fortress, strong and good.

Let responsibility be our call,
To nurture dreams, and stand up tall.
Like eagles, fierce in their defense,
We'll guard our goals, with diligence.

So take a cue from the eagle's might,
Be free, be focused, hold on tight.
With wings of purpose, hearts ablaze,
We'll claim our skies, in brighter days.

Owl

With eyes unblinking, wisdom sings,
The owl perched high on silent wings.
He sees the whole, the dark and light,
A patient soul who reads the night.

Let knowledge be our endless quest,
To see beyond, to learn the best.
Like owls, with vision sharp and keen,
We'll pierce the veil, the unseen glean.

When shadows fall, and whispers creep,
The owl's keen ears the secrets keep.
He listens deeply, understands,
The silent language of distant lands.

Let empathy be our guiding hand,
To hear the unheard, across the sand.
Like owls, with senses open wide,
We'll bridge the gaps, with hearts inside.

Through moonlit nights, he takes his flight,
A silent guide, a beacon bright.
He navigates by starlit sky,
A constant course, where dreams can fly.

Let purpose be our guiding star,
To chart a path, however far.
Like owls, with focus, clear and true,
We'll reach our goals, dreams coming through.

So learn from wisdom's watchful gaze,
See all, hear all, through life's maze.
With knowledge, empathy, and aim,
We'll reach new heights, and fan life's flame.

Hawk

The Hawk soars high, on currents of air,
A silent hunter, beyond compare.
With keenest vision, piercing through,
He spots his purpose, strong and true.

**Let perspective be our guiding sight,
To see the whole, with all our might.**

Like hawks, observing from the blue,
We'll grasp the bigger picture, in all we do.

With powerful talons, swift and precise,
He seizes chances, in a sudden vice.
Decisive action, no hesitation's plea,
A master of moments, wild and free.

Let decisiveness be our focused mind,
To act with purpose, leaving doubt behind.
Like hawks, striking with a sudden burst,
We'll seize opportunities, putting ourselves first.

Though solitary often, a majestic flight,
He guards his territory, with all his might.
A watchful presence, strong and bold,
His self-reliance, a story told.

Let independence be our inner core,
To stand alone, and ask for more.
Like hawks, soaring, strong and free,
We'll forge our own path, for all to see.

So take a lesson from the soaring hawk's grace,
Gain perspective, act, and find your own space.
With keen insight and a spirit so bold,
You'll master your destiny, a story untold.

Secretarybird

The Secretarybird, with long, elegant stride,
Through African savannas, he's a dignified guide.
With crested head and sweeping plume,
He hunts with purpose, dispelling gloom.

Let dignity be our elegant stance,
To walk with purpose, taking every chance.
Like Secretarybirds, graceful and so tall,
We'll face the world, standing up for all.

With powerful kicks, he strikes his prey,
A decisive hunter, throughout the day.
No hesitation, no fearful pause,
He lives by instinct, nature's wise laws.

Let decisiveness guide our every act,
To move with purpose, keeping on track.
Like Secretarybirds, swift and so precise,
We'll seize our moments, without thinking twice.

He builds his nest, high in the trees,
A watchful guardian, borne on the breeze.
For his young brood, a diligent care,
Protecting fiercely, beyond compare.

Let diligence be our constant aim,
To nurture what's vital, playing life's game.
Like Secretarybirds, attentive and true,
We'll care for our purpose, me and you.

So take a lesson from the Secretarybird's grace,
Be dignified, decisive, and find your own space.
With purposeful action and a diligent heart,
You'll play your essential, dignified part.

Osprey

The Osprey plunges, swift and bold,
A fish in talons, a story told.
From lofty perch, with piercing stare,
He spots his target, beyond compare.

**Let precision be our focused aim,
To strike with accuracy, in life's grand game.**

Like Ospreys, zeroing in with keenest eye,
We'll hit our marks, beneath the sky.

With powerful wings, he lifts his prize,
Through wind and weather, bravely he flies.
A solitary hunter, skilled and grand,
Master of his domain, across the land.

Let self-reliance be our soaring grace,
To achieve our goals, at our own pace.
Like Ospreys, independent and so free,
We'll forge our path, for all to see.

He builds his nest, a towering mound,
On lofty platforms, safe and sound.
For family he toils, with careful hand,
Protecting future, across the land.

Let dedication fuel our steady might,
To build for futures, shining bright.
Like Ospreys, laboring for their young,
We'll serve our purpose, a song unsung.

So take a lesson from the Osprey's flight,
Be precise, self-reliant, with all your might.
With focused passion and a steady aim,
You'll conquer challenges, in life's grand game.

Baza

The Baza, with crest held high and keen yellow eye,
Perches conspicuously, beneath a wide sky.
A slender raptor, graceful and alert,
Observing its world, avoiding all hurt.

Let keen observation be our focused art,
To notice details, and play a wise part.

Like Bazas, with piercing, watchful gaze,
We'll understand life, in its intricate maze.

Through dense canopy, it glides with such ease,
Or plunges swift, on a passing breeze.
Omnivorous tastes, it adapts to the fare,
Resourceful in hunting, beyond compare.

Let adaptability be our fluid grace,
To thrive in change, at our own pace.
Like Bazas, versatile, sleek, and so quick,
We'll find our footing, with every new trick.

Though often alone, or in pairs they fly,
Sometimes in flocks, beneath the vast sky.
A social gathering, before they disperse,
A momentary bond, to converse.

Let flexible connection define our way,
To join with others, for a brief display.
Like Bazas, communal, then on their own,
We'll find our balance, where we have grown.

So take a lesson from the Baza's sharp mind,
Be observant, adaptable, and gracefully kind.
With clear perception and a versatile soul,
You'll navigate life, making yourself whole.

Kite

The Kite, it circles, graceful and high,
A buoyant hunter against the sky.
With effortless loops and wings spread wide,
He rides the currents, with nothing to hide.

Let grace be our movement, fluid and free,
To navigate life, for all eyes to see.

Like Kites, with effortless, soaring flight,
We'll glide through challenges, bathed in light.

With watchful eye, he scans the ground,
For slightest movement, without a sound.
A master of patience, waiting for the breeze,
Seizing the moment, with quiet ease.

Let patience be our steady art,
To bide our time, and play a wise part.
Like Kites, observing with calmest gaze,
We'll seize opportunities, in life's slow maze.

Often seen soaring in a collective display,
A sky filled with dancers, come what may.
Though independent, they rise as a group,
A shared freedom, in a collective swoop.

Let shared purpose lift us, high and true,
To find common ground, for me and you.
Like Kites, together, in synchronized flight,
We'll achieve our goals, with all our might.

So take a lesson from the soaring Kite's way,
Be graceful, patient, and seize each day.
With collective spirit and a watchful eye,
You'll master your journey, beneath the sky.

Buzzard

The Buzzard circles, high above,
A patient watcher, born of love
For nature's cycle, stark and true,
He cleanses land, for me and you.

Let acceptance be our open mind,
To take what's given, leaving naught behind.

Like buzzards, finding purpose in decay,
We'll make the most of every single day.

With broad, dark wings, he rides the thermal's grace,
A master of efficiency, finding his space.
No wasted effort, no frantic chase,
Conserving energy, at his own slow pace.

Let efficiency guide our every deed,
To act with purpose, planting every seed.
Like buzzards, soaring with minimal strain,
We'll conserve our strength, through sun and rain.

Though often solitary in flight,
They gather sometimes, sharing the light.
A quiet company, a shared repast,
Their silent presence, built to last.

Let peaceful coexistence be our plea,
To share the world, for all to see.
Like buzzards, accepting and serene,
We'll find our harmony, on life's wide scene.

So take a lesson from the buzzard's flight,
Accept what is, and live with humble might.
With efficient spirit and a peaceful heart,
You'll play your essential, cleansing part.

Vulture

The Vulture perches, ancient and grand,
A silent sentinel across the land.
With bald, keen head and patient gaze,
He finds his purpose, in sunlit haze.

Let acceptance be our clear embrace,
To find purpose, in life's diverse space.

Like vultures, taking what the earth bestows,
We'll find our meaning, where true wisdom grows.

He cleanses all, with vital grace,
A necessary role, in nature's place.
No judgment cast, no turning away,
He serves his function, each passing day.

Let humility guide our actions true,
To serve a purpose, for me and you.
Like vultures, vital though misunderstood,
We'll contribute greatly, doing what we should.

Circling high, in effortless flight,
He spots his bounty, with keenest sight.
A patient watcher, soaring free,
Efficiently living, for all to see.

Let efficiency streamline our every stride,
To make the most of moments, with nothing to hide.
Like vultures, riding thermals, light and so grand,
We'll conserve our energy, across the land.

So take a lesson from the vulture's role,
Accept your purpose, making yourself whole.
With humble spirit and an efficient way,
You'll bring balance to life, each and every day.

13

Waterfowl and Seabirds

*Swan, Seagull, Penguin, Pelican,
Flamingo, Duck, Booby*

Swan

Upon the water, graceful glide,
A swan, serene, with mirrored pride.
Its feathers white, a glistening crest,
A picture of elegance, put to the test.

Let calmness be our guiding force,
To weather storms and find our course.
Like swans, on waters ever still,
We'll find our peace, with gentle will.

Beneath the surface, unseen power,
Paddling strong, through any hour.
Their hidden strength, a mystery,
A force beneath tranquility.

Let resilience be our inner fire,
To overcome, and rise ever higher.
Like swans, with grace that masks their might,
We'll face our struggles, take to flight.

In pairs they bond, a love so deep,
A lifelong vow, secrets they keep.
Their loyalty, a constant thread,
Two graceful souls, forever fed.

Let partnership be our heart's desire,
To find a love, that sets our soul on fire.
Like swans, in graceful, mirrored flight,
We'll build a love, ever so bright.

So take a lesson from the swan's display,
Find inner peace, and light the way.
With strength and love, forever true,
We'll glide through life, just me and you.

Seagull

With piercing eyes and piercing cries,
The seagull calls, across the skies.
A fearless soul, a brash ballet,
They fight for scraps, come what may.

Let tenacity be our guiding force,
To chase our dreams, and carve our course.
Like seagulls, bold and unafraid,
We'll face the challenges life has made.

They wheel and dive in playful fight,
A tireless dance, in morning light.
They find their joy in every squall,
Embracing life, and giving their all.

Let resilience be our inner strength,
To bounce back up, at any length.
Like seagulls, weathered by the storm,
We'll find our wings, and keep us warm.

Though scavengers they may appear,
They're part of nature's cycle, clear.
They clean the shores, a vital role,
A messy grace, that makes them whole.

Let resourcefulness be our key,
To find our worth, in all we see.
Like seagulls, using every scrap,
We'll find our purpose, never a gap.

So take a cue from the seagull's cry,
Be bold, be strong, and reach for the sky.
With tireless spirit, ever bright,
We'll find our place, and take to flight.

Penguin

With tuxedo sleek and waddle so bold,
The penguin marches, braving the cold.
On icy shores they huddle in tight,
A colony strong, bathed in pale light.

Let community be our guiding hand,
To build a warmth, across the land.
Like penguins, close in feathered embrace,
We'll find our strength, in every space.

They dive with grace, beneath the waves,
Expert hunters, nature enslaves.

With lightning speed and wings unseen,
They catch their prey, a glistening sheen.

Let perseverance be our aim,
To chase our goals, and fan life's flame.
Like penguins, diving deep and true,
We'll reach our dreams, with hearts anew.

They stand on guard, with watchful eyes,
Protecting chicks, beneath the skies.
With gentle care and tireless might,
They nurture young, in day and night.

Let dedication be our guiding star,
To love and cherish, no matter how far.
Like penguins, parents ever true,
We'll build a future, just for you.

So take a page from the penguin's plight,
Be strong, be warm, and hold on tight.
With purpose, love, and hearts that care,
We'll face the world, a future to share.

Pelican

A wonderful bird, with a pouch grand and wide,
The pelican soars, by the ocean's side.
With graceful dives and a wingspan so vast,
A fisher supreme, a creature built to last.

Let purpose guide you, on currents so strong,
Know your direction, where you belong.
Like pelicans, skimming the waves so blue,
Find your passion, and see it all through.

Their beaks they fill, a cavernous hold,
Enough for a feast, a story untold.

They share with their young, with care and with love,
A symbol of bounty, from the heavens above.

Let generosity be your guiding light,
To share your gifts, with all your might.
Like pelicans, feeding their chicks with glee,
Spread kindness outward, for all to see.

They gather in flocks, on sandy white shores,
A social bunch, where laughter soars.
With playful dives and synchronized flight,
A joy for life, a beautiful sight.

Let community be your guiding hand,
To build a bond, on shifting sand.
Like pelicans, in a feathered embrace,
Find strength in unity, and a cherished space.

So take a cue from the pelican's grace,
Be bold and generous, leave a positive trace.
With purpose clear and a heart that takes flight,
Soar through life's journey, bathed in golden light.

Flamingo

In pink plumage, tall and grand,
The flamingo wades on salty sand.
On single leg, they stand serene,
A graceful pose, a vibrant scene.

Let balance be our guiding light,
In work and rest, in day and night.
Like flamingos, poised with perfect grace,
We'll find our center, find our place.

With hooked beaks, they sift and strain,
For tiny prey in crimson rain.

They work together, side by side,
A patient hunt, where none can hide.

Let collaboration be our aim,
To share the load, and fan the flame.
Like flamingos, in a vibrant line,
We'll work as one, our goals entwine.

In vibrant flocks, they paint the sky,
A dazzling show, that catches the eye.
They move as one, a swirling tide,
A symphony in pink, they glide.

Let unity be our strength untold,
A tapestry of hearts, brave and bold.
Like flamingos, a feathered sea,
We'll stand together, eternally.

So take a page from the flamingo's grace,
Be balanced, work as one, find your space.
With vibrant spirit, hearts aflame,
We'll build a world, where all have a name.

Duck

The Duck, on water, floats with serene grace,
Paddling unseen, beneath the surface.
Calm on the top, with bustling feet below,
He navigates currents, with steady flow.

Let serenity be our outward calm,
While working diligently, safe from harm.
Like ducks, composed upon the pond,
We'll strive with effort, making a strong bond.

With feathers oiled, he sheds the rain,
Resilient spirit, again and again.
From water's dive to land's soft tread,
He adapts to changes, never dread.

Let adaptability be our gentle art,
To find our footing, playing every part.
Like ducks, at home in diverse terrain,
We'll adjust to changes, through joy and pain.

In quacking chorus, they greet the day,
A social family, in playful way.
Protecting ducklings, with watchful eye,
A loyal kinship, beneath the sky.

Let community be our joyful call,
To gather with others, standing up tall.
Like ducks, in flocks, so strong and true,
We'll find our solace, me and you.

So take a lesson from the duck's quiet might,
Be serene, adaptable, and join the light.
With tranquil spirit and a social heart,
You'll play a harmonious, essential part.

Booby

The Booby plunges, a swift, blue streak,
Into ocean depths, fish he does seek.
With aerodynamic form, he dives with might,
A focused hunter, a breathtaking sight.

Let precision be our focused drive,
To hit our targets, and truly thrive.
Like boobies, accurate in their aim,
We'll master our skills, in life's grand game.

On rocky ledges, in crowded array,
They gather in colonies, day by day.
A noisy community, close and tight,
Sharing the space, with all their might.

Let camaraderie be our joyful tie,
To live together, beneath the sky.
Like boobies, thriving in their collective space,
We'll build strong bonds, with warmth and grace.

Though clumsy on land, in air they are grand,
Soaring gracefully, across the land.
Adapting their movements, with powerful wings,
To different mediums, joy it brings.

Let versatility be our active quest,
To excel in diverse roles, putting us to the test.
Like boobies, at home in air and sea,
We'll embrace new challenges, wild and free.

So take a lesson from the booby's bold plunge,
Be precise, communal, and able to lunge.
With focused effort and a versatile soul,
You'll play your unique, magnificent role.

14

Flightless Birds

Ostrich, Cassowaries, Emu

Ostrich

With long necks and feathers soft,
Ostriches roam the open lot.
They run with speed, they jump with grace,
A sight to see, a wondrous race.

Let speed be our ally in flight,
To reach our goals, with all our might.
Like ostriches, swift and free,
We'll soar through life, with victory.

When danger strikes, they do not hide,
They stand their ground, with courage tried.

Their powerful kicks can foes defeat,
A strength to match, a will to meet.

Let courage be our shield and sword,
To face our fears, with hearts unstored.
Like ostriches, strong and brave,
We'll overcome, whatever the wave.

They work together, in family bands,
A bond of trust, that understands.
They share the load, they protect each other,
A love that's strong, like no other.

Let unity be our guiding light,
To stand together, in love and might.
Like ostriches, in family strong,
We'll face the world, and never go wrong.

So take a page from the ostrich's book,
Be fast, be brave, and united look.
With speed and courage, hearts ablaze,
We'll write our story, in brighter days.

Cassowaries

With casque like helmet, feathers brown,
The cassowaries stride, on ancient ground.
Flightless giants, with piercing stare,
Through rainforest depths, they tread with care.

Let resilience be your guiding light,
To weather storms, and hold on tight.
Like cassowaries, through changing times,
Adapt and thrive, in nature's rhymes.

They forage fiercely, with claws so strong,
Unearthing treasures, all day long.
Fruits and fungi, a jungle feast,
A vital role, for every beast.

Let resourcefulness be your call,
To find solutions, big and small.
Like cassowaries, through tangled maze,
Find what you need, in nature's daze.

Though solitary paths they roam,
Mates fiercely guard, their cherished home.
With watchful eyes and parenting pride,
They raise their chicks, with love inside.

Let loyalty be your guiding hand,
To cherish those in shifting sand.
Like cassowaries, strong and true,
Protect your loved ones, me and you.

(A threatened species, numbers fall,
Habitat lost, a mournful call.
Let's protect their home, from human greed,
The cassowaries, a timeless breed.)

So take a page from the cassowary's might,
Be strong, resourceful, hold on tight.
With purpose clear and hearts that beat,
Protect the jungle, a verdant retreat.

Emu

The Emu strides, with powerful leg,
Across the plains, with nary a beg.
A flightless wonder, tall and grand,
He journeys far, across the land.

Let perseverance be our steady gait,
To keep on moving, no matter our fate.
Like emus, striding through the wild,
We'll reach our goals, unbegged, unriled.

With curious eye, he pecks and gleans,
From varied bounty, through changing scenes.
Adapting diet, with clever mind,
What serves his purpose, he will find.

Let adaptability be our flexible thought,
To find new ways, expertly wrought.
Like emus, resourceful in what they eat,
We'll thrive in challenges, bittersweet.

Though often solitary, or in loose array,
They group for safety, at close of day.
A quiet understanding, a shared terrain,
Through life's vast journey, sunshine and rain.

Let self-sufficiency be our inner core,
Yet open to others, and asking for more.
Like emus, independent, but not alone,
We'll build our strength, on a steady throne.

So take a lesson from the emu's bold stride,
Be persevering, adaptable, with nothing to hide.
With steadfast spirit and a curious gaze,
You'll navigate life's ever-changing maze.

15

Colorful and Songbirds

Peacock, Tufted Titmouse, Hummingbird, Woodpecker, Toucan, Parrot, Pigeon, Dove

Peacock

With vibrant plumes in dazzling show,
The peacock struts, a radiant beau.
His tail unfolds, a starry night,
A breathtaking sight, a glorious light.

Let confidence be our inner flame,
To own our worth, and play life's game.
Like peacocks, proud in every hue,
We'll let our talents shine right through.

But beauty fades, as seasons turn,
New feathers grow, a lesson learned.

The peacock sheds, and starts anew,
Embraces change, with skies of blue.

Let growth be constant, ever bright,
To shed old ways, and greet the light.
Like peacocks, molting, ever bold,
We'll transform dreams, as stories unfold.

A hundred eyes adorn his train,
A watchful gaze, warding off pain.
The peacock sees, with senses keen,
The world's true nature, what's yet unseen.

Let awareness be our guiding force,
To see ourselves, and chart our course.
Like peacocks, with a watchful eye,
We'll navigate life, and learn to fly.

So take a cue from peacock's flair,
Embrace your strength, and what you wear.
With confidence, growth, and mindful sight,
We'll paint our world, ever so bright.

Tufted Titmouse

A crested head, a watchful eye,
The tufted titmouse soars on high.
Through branches dense, it flits and weaves,
A tireless soul, among the leaves.

Let perseverance be our guide,
To face each hurdle, stride by stride.
Like tufted titmice, ever bold,
We'll conquer challenges, new and old.

Their cheery song, a whistled tune,
Rings out each morn, beneath the moon.

A burst of joy, for all to hear,
Dispelling shadows, casting out fear.

Let optimism be our morning light,
To greet the day, with spirits bright.
Like tufted titmice, songs ablaze,
We'll find the sunshine, through life's maze.

With nimble feet and sharpest beak,
They glean their bounty, strong and unique.
Resourceful hunters, keen and quick,
They find what's needed, with every trick.

Let resourcefulness be our art,
To find what's needed, play our part.
Like tufted titmice, never lost,
We'll seek solutions, at any cost.

So take a lesson from the feathered friend,
Be bold, stay happy, 'til the very end.
With tireless spirit, hearts alight,
We'll face life's challenges, and take to flight.

Hummingbird

A jewel aloft, a whirring flight,
The hummingbird, a dazzling sight.
With wings a blur, a buzzing gem,
A tiny dancer, nature's diadem.

Let wonder be your guiding light,
To see the magic, day and night.
Like hummingbirds, on nectar sweet,
Find life's small joys, beneath your feet.

They sip from blooms, a hovering kiss,
A splash of color, pure bliss.

From flower to flower, a vibrant dance,
A tireless spirit, taking chance.

Let passion be your guiding flame,
To chase your dreams, and fan life's game.
Like hummingbirds, with hearts alight,
Pursue your goals, with all your might.

Though small in stature, wings so frail,
Their courage gleams, a valiant tale.
They face the wind, with fearless grace,
A tiny hero, in nature's space.

Let bravery be your inner call,
To stand up tall, despite the fall.
Like hummingbirds, on breezes bold,
Weather the storms, with hearts of gold.

So take a page from the hummingbird's might,
Be small but mighty, take to flight.
With curious minds and spirits free,
Find beauty's touch, eternally.

Woodpecker

With drumming beak and crimson crest,
The woodpecker works, to build its nest.
A tireless hammer, on a wooden wall,
Echoes ring out, a carpenter's call.

Let diligence be your guiding light,
To work with passion, day and night.
Like woodpeckers, focused, strong, and keen,
Craft your goals, a future foreseen.

They peck and prod, with focused might,
Unearthing treasures, hidden from sight.

Grubs and insects, their tasty prize,
A well-earned feast, beneath the skies.

Let perseverance be your guide,
To face the challenges, stride by stride.
Like woodpeckers, patient, pecking true,
Break through the surface, and see things through.

Though solitary in their quest,
Their drumming calls, put others to the test.
A message sent, a territory claimed,
Respect demanded, a game unnamed.

Let confidence be your guiding hand,
To stand your ground, and make a stand.
Like woodpeckers, loud and clear they say,
This is my path, I'll find my way.

So take a lesson from the pecking sound,
Be diligent, strong, and make your ground.
With focused hearts and tireless beat,
You'll carve your future, oh so sweet.

Toucan

With beak of sunshine, bold and bright,
The toucan flits, a dazzling sight.
Rainbow colors, feathers dressed,
A jester of the jungle, putting all the rest to the test.

Let vibrancy be your guiding light,
Embrace your colors, take to flight.
Like toucans, loud and oh so bold,
Show off your talents, never fold.

They squawk and chatter, high in trees,
A social bunch, a gentle breeze.

Sharing fruit with playful calls,
Friendship's laughter through the forest walls.

Let connection be your guiding hand,
Build lasting bonds, across the land.
Like toucans, perched in noisy throngs,
Find your tribe, where laughter belongs.

Their giant beak, a curious sight,
Holds hidden chambers, light and tight.
A marvel of design, unique and strong,
Nature's engineering, in its wondrous song.

Let curiosity be your guiding star,
Explore the world, however far.
Like toucans, peeking, bright and keen,
Uncover secrets, unseen, unseen.

So take a cue from the toucan's glee,
Be bright, be loud, and forever free.
With vibrant spirit and laughter's chime,
Fill the world with joy, one happy rhyme.

Parrot

The Parrot perches, with colors so bright,
A vibrant splash, a joyful sight.
With clever beak and agile claw,
He learns and mimics, breaking every law.

Let expressiveness be our joyful art,
To show our true colors, playing our part.
Like parrots, vivid and so grand,
We'll share our spirits, across the land.

With vocal talent, he learns to speak,
Mimicking sounds, lessons he does seek.
A keen observer, listening well,
Unlocking wisdom, a story to tell.

Let teachability be our open ear,
To absorb new knowledge, banishing fear.
Like parrots, learning every sound,
We'll grow in wisdom, on fertile ground.

In lively flocks, they chatter and play,
A social tapestry, throughout the day.
Protecting kin, with watchful eye,
A loyal kinship, beneath the sky.

Let camaraderie be our vibrant call,
To gather with others, standing up tall.
Like parrots, thriving in their happy crew,
We'll build strong friendships, me and you.

So take a lesson from the parrot's bright hue,
Be expressive, teachable, and loyal and true.
With joyful spirit and a learning mind,
You'll leave your mark, for all mankind.

Pigeon

On city streets, a constant hum,
he pigeon coos, a feathered chum.
They navigate the concrete maze,
Adaptable, in countless ways.

Let resourcefulness be our guide,
To make the most, with what's inside.
Like pigeons, find a hidden seed,
From scraps and challenges, we'll succeed.

With keenest eyes, they spot a crumb,
No detail missed, they never succumb.
Observant hearts, they take it all,
A wealth of knowledge, standing tall.

Let awareness be our open mind,
To see the world, of every kind.
Like pigeons, perched on window sill,
We'll watch and learn, with focused will.

They gather close, in flocks they fly,
A social network, reaching high.
Together strong, they find their way,
Through bustling crowds, each passing day.

Let community be our bond,
In friendship's warmth, we'll all respond.
Like pigeons, sharing what they find,
We'll build each other, heart and mind.

So take a lesson from the pigeon's flight,
Be resourceful, aware, and hold on tight.
With open eyes and helping hand,
We'll navigate life's promised land.

Dove

With wings of white, a gentle soul,
The dove takes flight, its message whole.
A cooing call, a peaceful plea,
For harmony's embrace, eternally.

Let kindness be our guiding star,
To show compassion, near and far.
Like doves, with feathers soft and light,
We'll spread goodwill, with all our might.

They build their nests in hidden nooks,
 haven safe, for gentle looks.
With patient care, they tend their young,
A love that's fierce, on loving tongue.

Let nurturing be our gentle touch,
To raise and guide, and love so much.
Like doves, with hearts that softly beat,
We'll nurture dreams, and make them sweet.

Through warring skies, they bravely fly,
A symbol of hope, that cannot die.
A fragile form, with spirit strong,
They carry peace, where wrongs belong.

Let perseverance be our fight,
For hope and peace, with all our might.
Like doves, enduring every test,
We'll strive for peace, and put it to the rest.

So take a wing from the dove's soft flight,
Be kind, be patient, hold on tight.
With gentle hearts and hopeful sighs,
We'll build a world, where peace never dies.

16

Unique Mammals

Hyena, Warthog, Platypus, Echidna

Hyena

With cackling laughs and spotted hide,
The hyenas prowl, with naught to hide.
They challenge lions, strong and bold,
In sisterhood, their story unfolds.

Let cooperation be our might,
To work as one, and share the light.
Like hyenas, clan above all else,
We'll find our strength, in stories we tell.

Their powerful jaws can crush the bone,
They hunt together, never alone.

With perseverance, they see it through,
A team that thrives, in loyal crew.

Let resilience be our inner core,
To face all trials, and ask for more.
Like hyenas, weathering life's storm,
We'll rise together, ever warm.

Though shunned by some, their laughter rings,
A joyful spirit, the freedom it brings.
Unafraid to be who they truly are,
They break the mold, shine bright, no matter how far.

Let authenticity be our guiding star,
To embrace ourselves, just who we are.
Like hyenas, laughing loud and proud,
We'll live our truth, in the voice unbowed.

So take a lesson from the laughing band,
Cooperate, fight, and make a stand.
With strength in numbers, hearts ablaze,
We'll find our voice, through life's many maze.

Warthog

With wart-faced grin and bristly mane,
The warthog grazes, sun and rain.
Though rough and tough, with tusks so bold,
It seeks out peace, a story untold.

Let resilience be our guiding light,
To weather storms, and hold on tight.
Like warthogs, strong through sun and rain,
We'll face life's blows, and rise again.

Beneath the hide, a heart so keen,
In mud they wallow, a cooling scene.

For mindful moments, they find their space,
A lesson learned, at a gentle pace.

Let self-care be our quiet time,
To soothe our souls, in peace sublime.
Like warthogs, wallowing in the mud,
We'll find our calm, where worries are subdued.

They root for truth with snouts so strong,
Unearthing facts where they belong.
With curious minds, they seek and find,
A thirst for knowledge, for all mankind.

Let curiosity be our guiding flame,
To ask, explore, and learn our name.
Like warthogs, digging deep and true,
We'll find new answers, born anew.

Though solitary paths they roam,
They form strong bonds, a place called home.
For family's sake, they fiercely stand,
United hearts, across the land.

Let loyalty with love entwine,
To cherish loved ones, make hearts shine.
Like warthogs, fierce in their defense,
We'll build a haven, with love immense.

So take a page from the warthog's plight,
Be strong, find peace, and hold on tight.
With curious minds and hearts ablaze,
We'll root out truth, through life's many maze.

Platypus

With duck-billed smile and webbed-foot stride,
The platypus glides, where waterside
And earth collide, a creature strange,
A furry fish, forever deranged.

Let mystery be your guiding light,
Embrace the odd, and hold on tight.

Like platypuses, defying form,
Find beauty yet, in the brewing storm.

Electric sensors grace their bill,
A hidden power, with subtle thrill.
They track their prey, unseen, unheard,
A silent hunter, with nature's word.

Let intuition be your call,
To sense the path, beyond the sprawl.
Like platypuses, with unseen might,
Navigate darkness, and find your light.

Venomous spurs, a hidden surprise,
A gentle creature, with a fierce disguise.
Duality reigns, in this curious friend,
A paradox swimming, that knows no end.

Let complexity be your embrace,
Layers unfold, with hidden grace.
Like platypuses, a puzzle untold,
Embrace the depths, of stories bold.

(They lay soft eggs, in burrows deep,
A mammal's nurture, secrets to keep.
Milk they produce, a wondrous feat,
A creature unique, oh so complete.)

So take a page from the platypus' might,
Be strange and strong, and hold on tight.
Defy all odds, with a quirky charm,
Leave lasting wonder, to keep us warm.

Echidna

The Echidna shuffles, with quills so keen,
A prickly presence, rarely seen.
With powerful claws, he digs with might,
Unearthing secrets, day and night.

Let protectiveness be our outward guard,
To shield our core, playing a strong card.
Like echidnas, bristling with defense,
We'll keep our true selves, with no pretense.

With long, sticky tongue, he finds his fare,
A specialized feeder, beyond compare.
Resourceful senses, in hidden ways,
Thriving quietly, through ancient days.

Let unique specialization be our guiding craft,
To hone our talents, a skillful shaft.
Like echidnas, with their distinct design,
We'll master our niche, truly divine.

A solitary wanderer, by choice he roams,
Building no grand, elaborate homes.
Content in self, in nature's wide embrace,
A quiet strength, in time and space.

Let self-reliance be our steady heart,
To find our comfort, playing our own part.
Like echidnas, independent and so free,
We'll build our peace, for all to see.

So take a lesson from the echidna's quiet way,
Be protective, specialized, each and every day.
With inward strength and a unique design,
You'll dig your own path, brilliantly shine.

17

Invertebrates - The Small but Mighty

Ant, Snail, Butterfly, Bee, Spider

Ant

The tiny ant, a mighty force,
In endless lines they chart their course.
With tireless work and selfless might,
They build a kingdom, bathed in sunlight.

Let diligence be our guiding light,
To strive for goals with all our might.
Like ants, we'll work with focused heart,
And build our dreams, a work of art.

Each has a role, a vital part,
No task too small, a beating heart.
Together strong, they lift the load,
A testament to teamwork on the road.

Let collaboration be our key,
For no one thrives in singularity.
Like ants, united, hand in hand,
We'll reach our peak, across the land.

Though small they seem, their strength profound,
They carry burdens many times their ground.
Persistence guides them, never quit,
They overcome all, with focused grit.

Let resilience be our inner core,
To face the setbacks, and rise once more.
Like ants, we'll weather every storm,
And find the sunshine, keeping us warm.

So take a cue from the ant's display,
Be hardworking, united all the way.
With focused hearts and spirits bold,
We'll build a future, more precious than gold.

Snail

A tiny house upon its back,
The snail goes slow, on mossy track.
A silver trail, a glistening sheen,
A patient traveler, on the forest scene.

Let perseverance be your guide,
Move with purpose, though the pace may chide.
Like snails, inching ever on,
Reach your goals, by the break of dawn.

They weather storms within their shell,
Safe and secure, where dangers dwell.

A quiet strength, a hidden might,
They wait it out, and see the light.

Let resilience be your inner call,
To weather hardships, big and small.
Like snails, enduring pounding rain,
Emerge renewed, to bloom again.

With gentle touch, they leave their trace,
A glistening path, a marked embrace.
Though small they seem, their mark they make,
A quiet presence, for goodness' sake.

Let kindness be your guiding hand,
Leave the world better, across the land.
Like snails, with gentle, glistening way,
Spread joy and beauty, every day.

So take a page from the snail's slow might,
Be patient, strong, and hold on tight.
With steady pace and gentle heart,
Leave shimmering trails, where you play your part.

Butterfly

With wings like stained glass, a fleeting sight,
The butterfly alights, a creature of delight.
From crawling form to beauty bright,
A transformation, taking flight.

Let change be our ever-guiding friend,
To grow and learn, until the very end.
Like butterflies, with wings unfurled,
We'll shed old skins, embrace a new world.

They flit from bloom to bloom with glee,
Sipping nectar, sweet and free.

A joy for life, in every beat,
Finding beauty, ever so sweet.

Let appreciation be our guiding light,
To savor moments, hold them tight.
Like butterflies, with hearts alight,
We'll find the joy, in morning's bright.

They dance on breezes, light and free,
A graceful waltz, for all to see.
A carefree spirit, taking hold,
A story whispered, yet untold.

Let joy be our ever-present guide,
To find the laughter, deep inside.
Like butterflies, with spirits bright,
We'll dance through life, with all our might.

So take a page from the butterfly's grace,
Embrace the change, find beauty's space.
With hearts that flutter, light and free,
Live a life joyful, eternally.

Bee

The Bee hums softly, a busy, golden gleam,
A tireless worker, part of a living dream.
From flower to flower, a diligent flight,
Gathering nectar, morning, noon, and night.

Let industriousness be our constant hum,
To work with purpose, till tasks are overcome.
Like bees, diligent, flying with grace,
We'll bring forth sweetness, in every place.

In complex hives, a marvel of design,
Each worker's role, perfectly divine.
A collective spirit, one goal they share,
For queen and colony, beyond compare.

Let cooperation be our guiding bond,
To build together, reaching far beyond.
Like bees, united, a living, buzzing stream,
We'll achieve great wonders, fulfilling every dream.

They dance their language, a message clear,
Sharing discoveries, banishing fear.
A clear communication, for all to know,
Where abundance flourishes, and good things grow.

Let communication be our open way,
To share our knowledge, each and every day.
Like bees, conversing with intricate art,
We'll build understanding, playing a vital part.

So take a lesson from the busy bee's flight,
Be industrious, cooperative, and shine so bright.
With shared purpose and a diligent heart,
You'll play a sweet, essential, productive part.

Spider

The Spider weaves, with intricate design,
A silken tapestry, subtly divine.
From slender thread, a trap so neat,
Patiently waiting, life's bitter-sweet.

Let creativity be our intricate art,
To spin new visions, playing a vital part.
Like spiders, weaving wonders from within,
We'll craft our futures, where true joys begin.

With silent steps, he knows his ground,
Feeling vibrations, without a sound.
A master builder, self-contained and keen,
Adapting structures, on every scene.

Let self-reliance be our steady hand,
To build our strengths, across the land.
Like spiders, independent and so true,
We'll craft our own paths, me and you.

Though often solitary, a mother's fierce guard,
Protects her egg sac, playing a strong card.
A silent devotion, deep and profound,
For future life, on hallowed ground.

Let protectiveness be our loving care,
To shield our precious, beyond compare.
Like spiders, guarding their tiny brood,
We'll keep our loved ones, understood.

So take a lesson from the spider's patient art,
Be creative, self-reliant, and play a loving part.
With intricate thought and a watchful eye,
You'll weave your own destiny, beneath the sky.

18

Life Aquatic - Fish

Koi, Seahorse, Shark, Ray

Koi

In pools serene, with dappled light,
The koi fish dance, a vibrant sight.
Scales like jewels, a rainbow gleam,
A silent ballet, in sunlit stream.

Let beauty be your guiding light,
Spread joy and wonder, day and night.
Like koi, with colors that enthrall,
Inspire the world, and stand up tall.

They glide and weave, a graceful form,
Overcoming currents, weathering the storm.

Resilience deep, in hearts of gold,
Finding their way, stories yet untold.

Let perseverance be your call,
To chase your dreams, and conquer all.
Like koi, ever swimming upstream,
Reach for your goals, a vibrant dream.

Legends whisper of wishes made,
As colored scales in sunlight fade.
A symbol of hope, and fortune's grace,
Bringing a smile to every face.

Let kindness be your guiding hand,
Spread joy and wonder, across the land.
Like koi, in schools that brightly gleam,
Build a community, a joyful team.

So take a cue from the koi's delight,
Be strong and graceful, hold on tight.
With shimmering scales and hearts alight,
Leave trails of beauty, ever bright.

Seahorse

With tail that grasps and body curled,
The seahorse sways, a wonder of the world.
Male or female, roles they share,
A partnership unique and rare.

Let interdependence be our guide,
To lift each other, with love inside.
Like seahorses, entwined and strong,
We'll build each other, where we belong.

They drift with currents, camouflage their form,
Blending with seagrass, safe from storm.

Adaptability's key they hold,
A lesson learned, in stories told.

Let flexibility be our art,
To bend and change, with open heart.
Like seahorses, in ocean's flow,
We'll find our way, wherever we go.

Though tiny creatures, hearts so bold,
They face the tide, their stories unfold.
With courage quiet, but ever true,
They navigate the ocean's blue.

Let resilience be our inner might,
To weather storms and rise with light.
Like seahorses, clinging to the tide,
We'll find our strength, deep inside.

So take a page from the seahorse's plight,
Be strong, adaptable, hold on tight.
With love that's shared and spirits free,
We'll dance through life's vast, endless sea.

Shark

The Shark glides silent, through ocean's deep,
A primal hunter, secrets to keep.
With senses sharp, to slightest tremor keen,
He navigates waters, a powerful scene.

Let instinct be our guiding force,
To trust our gut, and chart our course.
Like sharks, attuned to subtle sign,
We'll follow promptings, truly divine.

In constant motion, restless and grand,
He dominates oceans, across the sand.
A relentless drive, for survival's call,
Adapting to currents, standing strong through all.

Let persistence be our tireless might,
To move forward always, day and night.
Like sharks, ever restless, seeking their way,
We'll pursue our goals, come what may.

Though often solitary, a few will school,
A shared purpose, a collective rule.
Efficient hunters, each plays its part,
A powerful unity, within the heart.

Let decisive action be our swift command,
To seize opportunities, across the land.
Like sharks, striking with precision and might,
We'll act with purpose, strong and bright.

So take a lesson from the shark's silent grace,
Be instinctive, persistent, and set your own pace.
With focused power and a decisive soul,
You'll navigate challenges, making yourself whole.

Ray

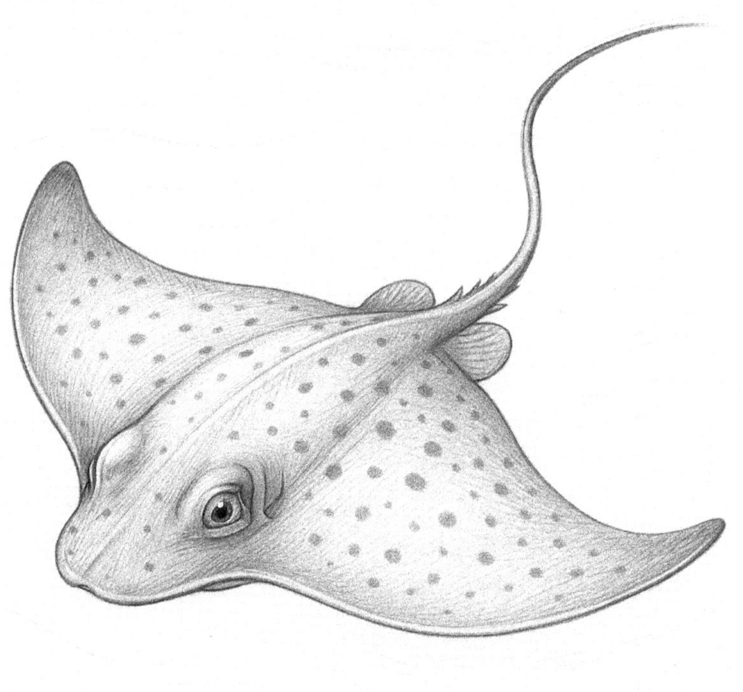

The Ray glides silent, a shadow wide,
Through sunlit shallows, where wonders hide.
With graceful undulation, free and deep,
He dances with currents, secrets to keep.

Let adaptability be our fluid grace,
To move with ease, in time and space.
Like rays, flowing with the ocean's sway,
We'll navigate changes, each and every day.

Beneath the sand, he finds his rest,
A camouflaged master, put to the test.
Patiently waiting, observing all around,
Content in stillness, on ocean's ground.

Let patience be our tranquil art,
To bide our time, and play a wise part.
Like rays, in stillness, hidden from view,
We'll wait for moments, strong and true.

With hidden barb, a silent might,
He guards his safety, day and night.
A defense reserved, for when in need,
Protecting self, planting a vital seed.

Let discernment be our careful way,
To use our power, in a thoughtful display.
Like rays, with measured, hidden sting,
We'll choose our battles, lessons they bring.

So take a lesson from the ray's soft glide,
Be adaptable, patient, with nothing to hide.
With tranquil spirit and a watchful gaze,
You'll navigate life's ever-changing maze.

Joel Hawksley is a distinguished veteran, author, entrepreneur, and community leader whose life has been shaped by his service to the country, commitment to professional excellence, and enduring passion for creative expression. During his 15 years in the US Army, he distinguished himself across multiple units and roles, leaving an indelible mark wherever he went. He was a paratrooper, a Military Policeman, and a Communication Specialist.

He transitioned to civilian life with the same tenacity and drive that defined his military career. Over the next twenty years, he developed a diverse portfolio of experiences in retail, education, politics, and entrepreneurship. Today, you can find him on podcasts, poetry readings, book signings, NASCAR races, public libraries, or at home writing and reading.